A Sexy Little Twist to Revitalize You and ReDesign Your Life!

Danne Reed

New York

fashionably LATE
A Sexy Little Twist to Revitalize You and ReDesign Your Life!

Published in New York, New York, by Morgan James Publishing. Morgan James and The Entrepreneurial Publisher are trademarks of Morgan James, LLC.
www.MorganJamesPublishing.com

The Morgan James Speakers Group can bring authors to your live event. For more information or to book an event visit The Morgan James Speakers Group at www.TheMorganJamesSpeakersGroup.com.

bitlit

A free eBook edition is available
with the purchase of this print book.

CLEARLY PRINT YOUR NAME ABOVE IN UPPER CASE

Instructions to claim your free eBook edition:
1. Download the BitLit app for Android or iOS
2. Write your name in **UPPER CASE** on the line
3. Use the BitLit app to submit a photo
4. Download your eBook to any device

ISBN 978-1-63047-578-9 paperback
ISBN 978-1-63047-579-6 eBook
Library of Congress Control Number:
2015902217

Cover and Interior Illustrations by:
Lauren Burke
www.HeyHeyDesigns.com

Cover Design by:
Rachel Lopez
www.r2cdesign.com

Interior Design by:
Bonnie Bushman
The Whole Caboodle Graphic Design

In an effort to support local communities and raise awareness and funds, Morgan James Publishing donates a percentage of all book sales for the life of each book to Habitat for Humanity Peninsula and Greater Williamsburg.

Get involved today, visit
www.MorganJamesBuilds.com

Habitat
for Humanity®
Peninsula and
Greater Williamsburg
Building Partner

Table of Contents

Introduction

The big 4-0 was like drinking a top-shelf martini from a paper cup. As I passed that milestone, I searched my life and saw some awe-inspiring things. My family was healthy and thriving; the business I was building with my husband was growing each year; and my net worth, while not enough to spring for a New York penthouse, was certainly sporting more black ink than it did in my twenties.

As I took stock, however, I also noticed a few gaping holes. Hey! Where was my passionate enjoyment of my work? Where was my dream home? Where was that best-selling book I had dreamed of publishing my entire life? And why the hell hadn't that vacation to Tuscany materialized yet? Someone had made a serious error, and I wanted to speak to their supervisor!

This was my reality at the time. To borrow a phrase from Stanley Ross and ABC, I knew the thrill of victory in some areas and the agony of defeat in others at the same time.

I had two options at this point. Truthfully, I'm sure there were more options, but I was at a low point, creatively speaking.

Option #1—A full-blown midlife crisis, complete with a bitter attitude, maxed-out credit cards, a string bikini made for a twenty-two-year-old (yikes!), and maybe even a scandalous affair with a younger man (I could've caught one if it was dark enough . . . or if he was on crutches). After all, I'd already missed the party, right? I was forty years old, and life hadn't handed me everything I wanted. Somehow, while I was busy doing the laundry and earning a living, my fabulous party of a life had fizzled out.

Or . . .

Option #2—I could just show up Fashionably Late! Rather than sitting around pouting over missing the party, sulking over what hadn't magically appeared thus far in my life, I could dust myself off and make a grand entrance. I could get back in touch with myself, rediscover what I *did* want, plan the most amazing party of a life, and make it happen. It was better than not showing up at all, and, possibly, maybe even better than showing up too early?

I know the suspense is killing you (and maybe my husband), so I'll tell you. I decided to show up for my life Fashionably Late! I introduced a Sexy Little Twist to my story plot and infused my life with a renewed sense of passion. So this is my life now . . . I showed up Fashionably Late, but the party is even better!

Incidentally, has your entire life ever changed in a sudden flash of clarity and understanding? Have you ever been completely transformed by a particularly insightful book or a charismatic speaker? Have you ever had a sudden epiphany that boosted you beyond your past and opened up your entire future?

Yeah, me neither.

I didn't have an "aha" moment. There was no epiphany or life-changing book or mind-altering speaker. It wasn't sudden or dramatic or marked by a spectacular event that I would later recognize as the line between my life before and my life after.

For me, it was more like a slow awakening. A process of coming to life after a long period of comfortable existence. A dawning of awareness and *inner knowing.*

As I look back now on this period of awakening, I can see that there are some life-changing and dramatic events that contributed to it.

There were joyful events—the awe-inspiring moments of watching my sons grow up, bringing my daughter home from China (and learning that she didn't have spina bifida after all), and growing a successful business with my husband.

There were challenging events—most significantly, the sudden and unexpected death of my mom. A rollover car accident that easily could have killed my son and me ("Mom said a bad word and then we went upside down!"). The surgical removal of pre-cancerous tissue and the breast cancer label of "high risk" (yes, I'm now a human pin cushion; and if that makes no sense to you, then consider yourself one lucky broad).

The point is that things didn't change overnight. The dramatic improvements in my life took place over the course of several years and, to a great extent and to my constant amazement, still are evolving (I didn't know how much I didn't know!).

I began searching for answers as to why, with so much to be grateful for in my life (healthy family, great marriage—though that was no accident, comfortable finances), I still felt that something was missing. I researched and studied and took courses and talked to people. I learned new techniques and tried new things and failed and tried more new things, and then read some more books. Eventually, I pieced together for myself the roadmap that you now hold in your hands.

Nothing can replace the knowledge gained from a journey of discovery, but we certainly can accelerate things by dropping you off nearer your destination. That is what this book will do for you.

And this, based on personal experience, is what you have to look forward to:

Before	After
Doubt about yourself and your ability to make things happen as you get older.	Acceptance of your brilliance, no matter what your age.
Areas of your life that are just not working for you.	Ongoing learning from new mistakes, but eliminating the actions that no longer serve you.
Seeming inability to attain goals that you know are vital to your happiness and well-being.	Ability to identify and eliminate self-sabotaging, subconscious thoughts and create empowering ones.

Low self-confidence and low self-respect.	High self-confidence and high self-respect.
Anxiety and helplessness about life in general, and a feeling that your life is happening "to" you and you can't change it.	Inner peace with the knowledge that you're capable of creating your life story.
Unaware and unappreciative of past successes.	Fully conscious of all the good decisions you've made in life.
Uncertainty about what you want to do with the rest of your life.	Perfect clarity on what you're meant to do with your life.
Fear of failing to use your talents and reaching the end of your life without ever *truly* living.	Passion and excitement with the knowledge of what your gifts are and how you'll serve others through their expression.
Defensiveness when your ideas and contributions aren't understood or appreciated.	No desire or need to convince anyone of your decisions or your path.
Sadness and a feeling of lack.	Gratitude and a feeling of abundance.
Unable to see a better future.	Re-awakening your imagination and using it to create your future.
Low energy.	High energy.
Tired, haggard, outdated appearance.	A look that beautifully expresses the person you are on the inside.
Resentment and anger toward loved ones when you're not happy. Resigned to feeling decidedly frumpy and outdated.	Amazing improvement in all relationships, with the grateful knowledge that you alone are responsible for your happiness. Excited to realize that you can be sexy at any age!

Will you achieve all of this by the end of this book? You certainly could! Chances are it will take some practice. But undoubtedly, you will have embarked upon a journey of personal discovery that has the power to transform the rest of your life, as well as the lives of those you touch, from your nearest and dearest loved ones to complete strangers on the other side of the globe.

Through discovery, exploration, and trial and error, I've created a Sexy Little Twist to my story by putting a little more of ME into the plot. All the elements of an amazing, joyful, fulfilling life are here. Have you created yours yet? Would you like to?

This book is a shortcut, since I've compiled the essential elements of transforming your life into one volume. Using this book, you'll be able to avoid searching for and arranging all the pieces of the puzzle. I've done that for you.

This book also is a roadmap. The steps to creating your dream life and then showing up for it are laid out in an order that will facilitate your learning and your growth.

This book is your Coach bag (since we're doing this in style) full of tools to help you succeed in adding a Sexy Little Twist to your life. You'll be able to reach into this book again and again for help if you get stuck.

And lastly, but most importantly, this book is your invitation. I'm looking for a few brave souls to join me in kicking complacency and resignation square in the teeth. Let's add a Sexy Little Twist and show up Fashionably Late to our lives!

Part I is a journey of discovery and hope. Your life until now, while great in some areas, doesn't exactly measure up to where you thought you'd be by this time. Something is missing. You know there's more out there for you, and you sincerely hope there's a way you can get your hands on whatever *it* is.

We'll take an honest look at what didn't work in the first part of your life and what's not working for you now. You're going to acknowledge the things that were unsuccessful so you can make adjustments. You'll recognize the parts of your life that are NOT YOU.

In short, a pep talk from a trusted friend would work wonders. The problem is that many of your friends are in the same situation, feeling the same way, and they don't know how to help.

Let me make this clear—you're not out of the game yet, sister! Part I will serve as your pep talk. By the end of Part I, you'll have more than a glimmer of hope that you can add a Sexy Little Twist to your life.

In Part II, you'll formulate a new strategy and create a sparkling new vision for your life. Showing up Fashionably Late to your own life requires a new way of looking at things. New beliefs are reinforced and anchored into a new mindset.

You'll finally acknowledge the many things you've done well so far (and yes, there are *many*). Once you give yourself credit for your successes, you'll realize you can use what you already know to boost your future efforts.

Strategies will be revealed. You'll revive some dormant knowledge and learn some new techniques that will help you prepare for your life with a Sexy Little Twist.

Part III will help you prepare for the "showing up" part of the equation—sharing the new you with the rest of the world. It all sounds fabulous in a book, but this is real life we're talking about and things come up.

You'll go back into action with a renewed sense of hope and enthusiasm, bolstered by some tangible tools, techniques, and behaviors for turning your life into a celebration.

Heads up—showing up Fashionably Late to your own life is not a spectator sport!

You'll want to get a notebook or journal (we'll call it your Sexy Little Twist journal) to complete the exercises presented in this book, take notes on things that grab you, and track your progress. Yep, this is more of a workbook than a coffee table book. Sorry 'bout that! But you're smart enough to realize that simply reading a book isn't going to change your life. It's the work you do, based on what you learn, that changes the game.

And for the quickest, most deeply transforming experience, gather some friends and work through the chapters together one week at a time. Each chapter includes all of the elements you'll need to make it fun and productive:

- Concepts and stories
- Exercises
- Sexy Little Twists (Chapter Takeaways)
- Girl Talk—Discussion questions for groups, or journal exercises if you're working alone

So invite the girls over for an evening and add a Sexy Little Twist to your lives! Remember that showing up Fashionably Late can be far more exciting than arriving too early or not showing up at all!

Let's get this party started!

Part I

Discovery and Hope

"Inside every older person is a younger person wondering what the hell happened."
—**Cora Harvey Armstrong**

Chapter 1

What's This about a Sexy Little Twist?

*"Every time I think I have all of my ducks in a row,
I turn around and one of those bitches is waddling off!"*
—Stevenhumour.com

Sexy

Just reading the word kind of makes you grin, doesn't it? The dictionary on my desk defines it as "tending to arouse sexual desire or interest." Wikipedia describes it simply as an adjective used to describe a sexually appealing person or thing. But it's so much more than that, isn't it?

What does *sexy* mean to you? There are as many definitions as there are individuals, since each of us has our own ideas, tastes, and preferences. Try Googling "sexy" sometime, and you'll see what I mean.

And yet, there are some ideas of *sexy* that we all generally agree upon, and I am referring to these intangible characteristics when I use the word.

From my research, here are a few traits that show up repeatedly in polls on the subject:

Confidence—that little something that says, "I'm me and I'm perfectly comfortable with that."

Sense of Humor—the ability to take things lightly, to laugh at circumstances and at oneself.

Determination—that fire within that keeps one from quitting when things get challenging.

Inner Calm—strength of conviction that lets others know that everything will be okay.

Wonder—the tendency to see the beauty in one's surroundings, in others, and in the world. Embedded in this characteristic is a sense of youth. Not necessarily a young body, because bodies age; but a youthful way of looking at the world, being open to new ideas and experiences.

Vitality—sexy is strong and vibrant and doesn't run out of steam when the job's half done, if you know what I mean. Seriously, there's an energy to being sexy.

I'm sure you can add others to this list, but for simplicity's sake, let's go with just those for now. Imagine all of these characteristics rolled into one person— someone with quiet confidence, determination, and inner calm, with energy, a sense of humor, and an appreciation for true beauty in the world.

Pretty sexy, right? I think so, too.

Now think back to a time in your adulthood when you possessed all of these characteristics at the same time.

No, really. Go ahead. I'll wait . . .

So, how far back did you have to go?

Was it when you were in your early twenties and just getting started? In your late twenties as a young mom? In your thirties and making progress in your career? Your forties and starting a new business? If it was just last week, by all means put this book back on the shelf and walk away. You're sexy already.

But if you're like me, you didn't really find a time in your adulthood when you were truly living ALL of them at the same time. I had to go back to my childhood to get them all at once. Do you remember that time in your childhood when you were full of confidence, laughter, determination, strength, and wonder? I do and when I realized I had lost some of it along the way, I wanted it back.

Little

When I set out to show up Fashionably Late, my life was already going well in some areas. I'm sure that yours is, too. We're not necessarily talking about a complete overhaul (though that's certainly doable if it's what you want).

Regardless of how far it is between where you are now and where you'd love to be, it's the little things that will get you there. The small steps you'll take each day will move you ever closer to living your best life.

Whether you believe it or not right now, you're not far from your ideal life. In fact, the more painful it is, the closer you are to it. It's frustratingly close; thus the pain of not having it is most acute.

Let the word *little* be your constant reminder that all you're doing is taking small steps back toward YOU, toward your true self.

Twist

What's a girl to do when she realizes she's lost a little of what made her amazing? All she needs is a little twist! For our purposes, three definitions apply:

1. A plot twist. A turn in the plot of a story, as in a radical change in the expected direction or outcome. Imagine cruising along, just like you always have, doing things the way you've always done them, getting the same mediocre results; and then, suddenly, "Whoa! What just happened? Did you see that? I was NOT expecting THAT!"

    I LOVE how this applies to transformation in life, whether it's in a single area, such as fitness or work, or an overall lifestyle change. It's so rewarding to continually surprise ourselves by what we can do. When we set out to peel back the layers and rediscover our authentic self, we find that we're capable of anything we ever dreamed. Makes for a fascinating, sexy plot twist! It's kind of fun to keep other people guessing, too.

2. A cocktail twist. Another favorite of mine—the kind that decorates and flavors a martini. It's just that little extra something that turns a dull, functional beverage into a celebration. Makes it taste better and, if you let it, brings a smile to your face.

   And that's exactly what the little changes in this book can help you do—bring more flavor and enjoyment to your life, turning your functional life into a party.

3. Last, but certainly not least, is a Twist of Fate—an unpredicted occurrence with far-reaching consequences. The little things that this book will inspire you to do will indeed have far-reaching consequences, far more than you can possibly imagine at this moment. Not only in your own life, but in the lives of everyone around you, even people you've not met and may never meet. That's the power and the force of YOU—the magic in you fulfilling your destiny.

So that's what I mean by a Sexy Little Twist. We're going to give your story, your destiny, a Sexy Little Twist by bringing back the bits of YOU that have been lost along the way, by showing up Fashionably Late to your own life!

Aimlessly Adrift

Let's begin with a story. Can you guess what the following people have in common?

Event planner, waitress, administrative assistant, quality consultant, corporate trainer, project manager, farmer, truck driver, bookkeeper, clinic administrator, hospital CEO, financial planner, writer, and life coach.

You've probably noticed that all are vocations, rather than actual people. Or you might have noted that each of these callings requires some level of expertise, efficiency, and time management skill. But that's not the answer I'm looking for.

The answer is *me*. At one time or another, I have made ends meet in each of these roles.

Now maybe you're saying to yourself, "No way she switched jobs that often." Or perhaps you can totally relate to this seemingly random background. Or maybe you're just thinking that I'm a total flake right now. Fair enough. Regardless, let me explain.

I left high school not knowing what I wanted to be when I grew up. *Not knowing* stayed with me for a long time. In fact, it stayed so long that at age forty, I began to worry that it would always be with me.

I wasn't particularly unhappy in any of these roles. I learned invaluable lessons and met amazing people along the way. But there's no denying that, with regard to my work life, I was drifting aimlessly. I was not taking charge of my direction. I was allowing circumstances to choose me, rather than the other way around.

Through it all, the nagging feeling that I was missing something important never eased. None of the hats that I tried on were a perfect fit. I was on a road to somewhere or something, but I didn't know where or what.

As a kid, I had big dreams about being shockingly wealthy and traveling the world doing work that I loved. At forty, I still was waiting to find out how all of this was going to come to pass. Seriously, I was hoping to *stumble upon* what I was meant to do with my life. In my game of life, the score was Not Sexy—One Point; Sexy—Big Fat Zero.

With the résumé you see listed above, I had yet to stumble upon my dream life and began to have doubts. I began to ask, "*Is this it? Is this all there is? What if there's nothing out there to 'stumble' onto?*" My greatest, most challenging, and rewarding role is that of mom, but kids don't stay little forever. *Were my greatest achievements all behind me?*

These were the questions that wiggled into my consciousness during rare quiet times (while driving to pick my kids up from school, waiting in line at the grocery store, those first few moments in the morning before my busy family got out of bed). Questions that had me a little on edge and kept me up at night. Questions that sometimes made themselves known in a twinge of resentment toward the very people I cared about the most.

And that, more than anything, snapped me out of it. The fear of gradually becoming a bitter, grouchy old woman was enough to shake me out of my funk and into action. I spent the next few years absorbing everything I could find about life purpose, happiness, success, late bloomers, building wealth, and even improving brain function, among other things.

What I discovered was that I could totally transform my life with a few Sexy Little Twists!

Since you've picked up this book, I'll assume that you, too, are asking questions and wondering if there is more to life than what you're experiencing. Maybe you're doing fabulously in many areas of your life, but your work isn't satisfying or engaging. Or perhaps your level of fitness is making you feel older than you are. Or maybe your career is going great, but your relationships leave something to be desired. Regardless of the details, your life isn't quite as fulfilling as you hoped it would be by this time. Deep down, you know there must be something more than what you're experiencing, and you're looking for a way to turn it around. You want to feel sexy again, like you're the leading lady in your own story!

Fashionably Late

So, just what does it mean to show up Fashionably Late to your own life?

It means that the very heart of any joyful, happy, successful life is the honoring and celebrating of the one who's living it! Your life is what you've made of it so far. It's functional. It works in many ways. But the parts of it that aren't working for you are the ones you've allowed others to throw in. What's lacking in it are the things you've allowed others to convince you to take out.

Showing up Fashionably Late to your own life is about keeping what you love and drop-kicking what you don't, and then adding Sexy Little Twists of your own passion, purpose, and style back in. You're the one who decides what stays and what goes. No one else. Just you.

Think about that for a moment. What would turn your functional life into a party? What is missing from it that would give it that tingly thrill that makes you want to hop out of bed in the morning? Don't remember the tingly thrill? What puts that sparkle in your eye? Has it been too long since you experienced it? Well, you're in luck! I have another metaphor for just such an occasion!

Think of the last time you saw an amazing turnaround by a sports team. If you can't think of one, use your imagination. Recall that when all seemed lost, the team pulled off a miracle and delighted you with a glorious victory, just when you had begun to brace yourself for a painful defeat.

Now apply that same heart-pounding, edge-of-your seat excitement to your life!

Let's face it—we'd all love to experience this kind of victory at some point in our lives. We all yearn to be a part of something noble and inspiring. How brilliant would it be if that something was our own life story?

As women, we're spouses, partners, parents, aunts, grandmothers, children, friends, bosses, coworkers, business owners, clients, church and community members, volunteers, and numerous other roles that have great influence on the lives of those around us. What does your life say to the people you encounter? Does it give them courage and hope? Does it inspire others to live out *their* dreams?

Our very nature as social creatures (we love to talk!) makes us remarkably suited to sharing our success with others. Realize and embrace the power you have to not only change yourself, but also to change the lives of everyone around you.

And really, what's not to love about finally sorting through the many experiences, beliefs, customs, and expectations of our life and choosing our path based on who we truly are?

Early in your life, there was a pure YOU who knew exactly what she wanted and loved. She's still in there, waiting for a shot at a joyful life. She's the one who asks, "*Is this it? Is this all there is?*" She's the one who's a tad disappointed with the outcome of the game so far.

Let's start a revolution. A Sexy Little Twist revolution. It all starts with YOU, at long last, showing up Fashionably Late to your own life. It all starts with a Sexy Little Twist of what you love and what you're passionate about. Who's with me?

Little Twists of Sexy:

1. Confidence, humor, determination, inner calm, and wonder are sexy!
2. The very heart of any joyful, happy, successful life is the honoring and celebration of the one who's living it.

3. If you feel like something is missing from your life, it's probably YOU.

4. If YOU *are* missing from your life, you can find YOU and put YOU back. YOU, only sexier.

Chapter 2

Believe in the Fashionably Late Entrance!

*"Nothing makes a woman more beautiful than
the belief that she is beautiful."*
—Sophia Loren

I f living your life with a Sexy Little Twist is the equivalent of being at the most joyful, fun party ever, then let's take a step out onto the terrace for a moment. It's a little quieter, and we can discuss something of a geekier nature—the science of a fulfilled life.

Yep, you read that right. Our potential to enjoy and celebrate our life fully has a scientific foundation. And we're going to explore it in order to employ it.

In his book *Biology of Belief*, Bruce Lipton puts out a genius idea that I had never really considered. Most people believe in the placebo effect—the very real phenomenon where patients recover from an illness simply because they believe

11

they're being given a treatment, whether that's in the form of drugs, surgery, or any number of other "fake" therapies. However, very few studies are conducted to examine *why* the placebo effect is so darn . . . effective. The people who are healed using a placebo are just as sick before the study as the people who are healed by taking the actual drug. It's not as if the study group healed by the placebo imagined their illness. And while we usually hear of the placebo effect in terms of physical healing, it applies equally to all aspects of our lives. So what is it that causes the healing to occur in a patient who is taking a sugar pill or receiving "fake" surgery?

A few years ago, I finally took action on a dream I'd had for a long time. I sat down and wrote a novel. Well, actually, it took about a year and a half to write. And when it was finished, I put the printed manuscript—all 325 pages of it—in a shoebox and shoved it into my closet under my slacks and behind my boots. And that's where it sits to this day.

You may be wondering why a person would go to all that trouble to write a book, only to hide it in a closet. Or maybe you're nodding your head right now because you have a similar project that you started and didn't follow through on. Either way, I can tell you that the pivotal element in this scenario, as it is in the placebo effect, is *belief*.

At the basic level, beliefs are thoughts that you accept as true. If you once had a thought that you were unattractive, and you accepted that thought as the truth, you likely developed the belief that you are unattractive. This wouldn't be a huge problem for you if you woke up one morning, looked in the mirror and thought, "I'm not that bad. I'm actually kind of pretty when I curl my hair and put on a little lip gloss."

However, if instead you held the "I'm unattractive" belief in your mind for an extended period of time, then your brain set to work helping you find (and create) other evidence to support the belief that you're unattractive—that boy next to you in science class doesn't even look your way, the neighbor lady scowls at you every morning when you walk by her house on the way to school, etc. This solidifies the "I'm unattractive" belief even further. Never mind that the boy in science class might just be super shy and the neighbor lady has a hangover every morning. Your brain, ever helpful to validate your beliefs, was looking for evidence that you were unattractive and found it for you. Thanks, brain!

If left unchecked, this unhelpful little belief becomes deeply and strongly rooted in your psyche. And what you are at this moment in time is an intricate web of thousands, maybe millions, of these beliefs that you've developed over the course of your life. This intricate web of beliefs makes up your belief system.

Just as we are supported by the physical systems in our body—respiratory, digestive, circulatory, nervous, and so on—we also are supported by our belief system. And just like our body's other systems, our belief system may be serving us well, or it may not.

In his book *Think Your Way to the Life You Want*, Bruce Doyle uses a diagram to show your original thought or belief as the trunk of a tree, with supporting thoughts and beliefs attaching to it like branches, strengthening the root thought.

For example, the original thought of "I'm not very smart" becomes the root belief when it's held for a period of time. Then other supporting thoughts begin to attach to it—"I'll never make it in college"; "I won't get the promotion"; or "I'll be overlooked at the awards ceremony." As each new belief attaches, the original belief of "I'm not very smart" gets validated and strengthened. I like to take this tree analogy a step further and liken it to the redwood trees in California. Through an elaborate root system, each belief (tree trunk) attaches to the other beliefs (nearby tree trunks) to create a huge organism of related and unrelated beliefs.

A belief about your overall intelligence connects to a belief about your ability to do well on tests, which connects to a belief about your ability to perform well in stressful situations, which connects to a belief about your ability to speak in front of an audience.

Using the "I'm not very smart" example, suddenly you're forty years old and you're in a cold sweat because you have to present a report to your boss's boss. What you don't realize is that you're still experiencing the effects of flunking a math test in second grade. Kind of crazy when you look at it like that, huh?

In the case of my novel, even after a year and a half of writing and dreaming and hoping, I still carried the belief that I couldn't publish a book. Somewhere in my belief system was the deeply rooted idea that I wasn't a good enough writer, didn't have enough connections, wasn't lucky enough, blah, blah, blah. So, into the closet it went!

Different Types of Belief

Beliefs can be conscious, meaning we're aware of them, or subconscious, meaning we are unaware of them. Dr. Wayne Dyer likes to use the word "habitual" rather than "subconscious." "Subconscious" implies that the belief is so deeply imbedded in our minds that we can't even get to it in order to work on it, like trying to change the settings on an iPhone that's locked inside a bank vault. "Habitual" is a more accurate and helpful term, since we absolutely *can* access our subconscious and make changes. But more on that shortly.

First, let's look at the difference between a conscious belief and a subconscious one. An example of a conscious belief might be when we say the following to a friend: "I am so bad at job interviews. I always get nervous and end up saying something that costs me the job." In this example, we are well aware that we believe we have the tendency to say something stupid during interviews.

On a subconscious level, that same belief might cause us to blurt out something inappropriate or reckless during a job interview. Then we walk away from it, shaking our head and thinking "Why on earth did I say that?"

Whether conscious or subconscious, this example is obviously a limiting belief rather than an empowering one. On the right is a diagram to illustrate the four types of beliefs:

Whether conscious or subconscious, the limiting beliefs are the ones that need to be eradicated if you are going to show up Fashionably Late to your own life! I like to call the beliefs on the right side of this diagram "passion assassins," because that is exactly what they do. They sneak up and annihilate all the joy in your life, sometimes without you even realizing it (as in the case of the subconscious/habitual ones). The death of your dreams may not be as sudden as being sniped; but they die nonetheless, over time, sadly and slowly.

So I say let's kill the passion assassins first! Once you eliminate them, creating the circumstances you choose to have in your life becomes much easier.

FOUR TYPES OF BELIEFS

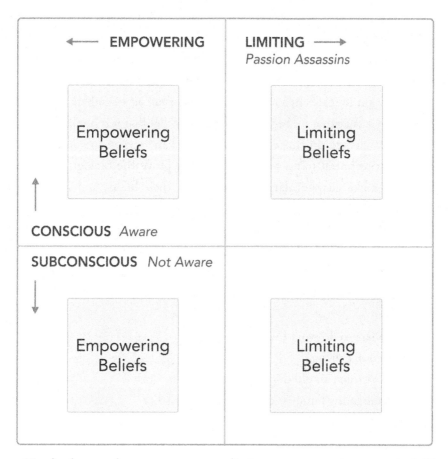

Here's the good news—you *can* eliminate your passion assassins! The subconscious ones will have to be brought into your awareness, or conscious mind, in order to address them; but you can do this, and I'll show you how.

First, you have to believe it can be done.

I have to confess that, until a few years ago, I believed that if I thought something, it must be true. I further believed that what I thought was true couldn't be changed until some external event proved to me otherwise. This goes back to the old saying "seeing is believing." My belief that my thoughts were always true was so strong that I would agonize over fleeting thoughts for long periods of time, trying to decipher what they might mean. Weird dreams would leave me puzzled and inwardly confused for half the morning.

The truth is that the mind can be a reckless, undisciplined little rascal until you learn to control it. And control it you can!

Of course, the first step in learning to control your mind, just like everything else, is to *believe* you can. Everything in your life begins with belief.

I don't want to scare anyone off, but it's important as we embark on our Sexy Little Twist journey that we begin with a strong belief that it is humanly possible to make this change. In this chapter, you'll find the layperson's description of some highly technical terms and concepts that prove the biological ability of humans to make changes, large and small, to their brains and bodies, and, therefore, their lives.

It's important that you're absolutely convinced that you can purposely change your brain and body before you'll be encouraged and motivated to do so.

Let's address some of the myths or misconceptions about aging. Have you ever heard or said any of the following:

"It's too late to do what I want to do."
"People don't change."
"You can't teach an old dog new tricks."
"Everyone in my family is overweight; it's genetic."
"If I would have known that when I was young, then I would have . . ."
"I can't afford to change careers now."
"If I do something different now, then I will have wasted my whole life."

Perhaps, like many people, you have heard some of these passion assassins, or even said some of them. Perhaps you even believe them, if only on a subconscious level. In this chapter, I'll show you how conventional scientific wisdom on aging, genetics, and healing is now being refuted.

Placebo Effect

Let's start with this one, since it's the most commonly known. I mentioned the concept of the placebo effect earlier in this chapter. In pharmaceutical studies, patients receiving sugar pills report the same level of healing as patients receiving the actual drug being tested. But have you heard about the study where patients received fake *surgery*? If not, brace yourself because this is a shocker!

In order to determine which part of arthroscopic knee surgery was actually effective, doctors in Texas divided patients with debilitating knee pain into three groups. The medical team scraped the knee joint of one group; the team "flushed" the knee joint in another group; and the third group received a "non-procedure" in which the surgical team made three incisions in the knee area and *pretended* to operate. I mean, picture that—the surgeon making actual incisions and then *pretending* to perform surgery. Probably would have been comical to watch.

But the joke's on the surgeons because two years later, the "fake surgery" patients in the third group reported the same amount of relief from pain and swelling as the patients in the first and second group who received the actual treatments. You've heard the ancient Roman poet Virgil's saying, "Love conquers all"? Well, in this scenario, as in many areas of life, *belief* conquered all. All of the patients *believed* the surgery would work, and so it did. I wonder if the patients paid the surgeon's bill in "fake" money. No matter, I'm sure they're not complaining either way.

The bottom line? Belief can change the outcome! And not just in our minds, but in our physical experience, in our bodies. The theory is that our thoughts have a vibration, a frequency that they send out, much like radio waves. We can't see them, but they're there, radiating out from our mind. And our cells actually *respond* and *change physically* according to those vibrations! When we send out the thought frequency that we're ill, and that we're not going to get better, our cells respond. When we send out the thought frequency that we're healthy, our cells start vibrating at that same frequency.

Given this, think about the impact, over time, of the belief that women naturally tend to gain weight as we get older. Are you falling victim to a passion assassin that's been ingrained in your belief system? Something to think about.

Now let's talk about how belief can affect what we notice on the outside, in our physical environment.

Reticular Activating System

This topic gets to the heart of your ability to see possibilities. One of the reasons we see the world the way we do is because of something in our brains called the Reticular Activating System (RAS). Through our senses, we are receiving millions of bits of data at any given time. Most of this data is ignored. For example, your left elbow is sending data to your brain at this very moment. However, until you read the words "left elbow" on the page, you probably were unaware of what you were feeling in your left elbow. As soon as you read the words "left elbow," your attention was drawn to it and you then noticed what you were feeling there.

Another common example of this is when you are thinking about buying or have just recently bought a particular kind of car. Suddenly, you see that same type of car everywhere, though you likely never noticed them before.

Your RAS causes this phenomenon. The RAS acts as a filter, allowing you to become aware only of that which you focus on and believe is possible.

So, what happens if you don't believe that you have the ability to lose weight? Or if you don't believe you can switch careers? Or buy a new house? Your brain will filter out any data that might show you otherwise. Anything that might support you in those endeavors would be filtered out by your RAS. Think of that! If you don't believe you can ever be a millionaire, then your RAS is, at this very moment, filtering out numerous methods for making a million dollars.

Here's a true story that illustrates the point—a woman actually tossed a one-million-dollar winning lottery ticket in the trash can at the convenience store where she bought it. She looked at it, didn't SEE what was right in front of her, and discarded it! What do you suppose was her underlying belief at that moment that caused her RAS to filter out a winning ticket?

So, what if we could turn that around? What if we taught our brain to believe that we could be millionaires? Winning lottery tickets aside, what if we taught our brain to believe that we could achieve our perfect weight, or find our perfect job, or discover our life's purpose?

What, you don't think you can teach your own brain? That's where our next concept comes in—neuroplasticity.

Neuroplasticity

Neuroplasticity is the brain's ability to change its structures and functions in a fundamental way. It has been a long-held belief in science that as we age, we lose the ability to change our brains. In other words, our brains become fixed and unchangeable. But recent studies have proven that this simply is not the case. In fact, studies are now showing that the overall conventional "wisdom" that our brains are unchangeable has likely been the very thing that keeps our brains from experiencing change. Ironic, isn't it?

In her book *Train Your Mind, Change Your Brain,* Sharon Begley cites a 1987 study on patients with Obsessive Compulsive Disorder (OCD). This study proved that mindfulness therapy (focusing on awareness of thought and feeling) could alter the brain. She stated that "mental action can alter the brain chemistry of an OCD patient. The mind can change the brain." And, thus, an "avenue to self-directed neuroplasticity" was realized. In other words, we can actively and deliberately change and improve the performance of our own brain. When you think about it, it's not all that farfetched. We have no trouble at all believing that we can improve the functioning of any other part of our body—heart, digestive system, respiratory system, etc. Why not our brain? Turns out, it's no different.

Dr. Daniel Amen, author of several best-selling books detailing his study of the brain, agrees. He takes pictures of brains using single photon emission computed tomography (SPECT), both before and after treatment, much of which is through natural means. The "after" pictures, even in the elderly, show a decidedly different brain than the "before" pictures. More importantly, his patients experience and report a remarkable difference in their lives. In fact, Dr. Amen feels strongly that any significant life change *must* start with a healthy brain. By improving our brain function, we not only can overcome problems like anxiety, depression, and addictions, but also can become more thoughtful, creative, energetic, focused, and effective. Briefly, the following are some of Dr. Amen's recommendations for improving the function of your brain:

- Make positive social connections.
- Engage in new learning.
- Maintain a healthy diet.

- Take a daily multiple vitamin.
- Take a fish oil supplement.
- Learn music.
- Exercise regularly.
- Dance (without excessive martinis).
- Engage in positive thinking.
- Express gratitude.
- Meditate.

We'll talk more about several of these topics later, but for now just consider that the health of your brain has a direct impact on your ability to succeed in any undertaking. Adding any of these activities to your daily routine can have a significant impact on the health of your brain.

I began this chapter with Bruce Lipton's insightful question about the placebo effect, and I'll end it with his wisdom as well.

There are two fields of science to which Dr. Lipton points in substantiating his research and ideas presented in *The Biology of Belief.*

The first is the science of *signal transduction*, which focuses on the biochemical pathways by which cells respond to environmental cues. Dr. Lipton states that environmental signals can, through cytoplasmic (cell casing) processes, alter how genes express themselves. Environmental signals thereby influence cell movement and even control cell fate—whether the cell lives or dies. This means that the fate and behavior of an organism is directly linked to its *perception* of its environment. And what are we if not an organism made up of billions and billions of these "environment-sensing" cells? What messages are you sending to your cells? In short, the character of our life is based largely upon how we perceive it.

The second field of science is a fairly new one called *epigenetics*, which literally means "control above the genes." This area of science is threatening to turn conventional genetic wisdom on its head. It's the science of how environmental signals select, modify, and regulate gene activity. With it comes the realization that our genes are constantly being remodeled in response to life experiences, which again emphasizes that our perceptions (beliefs) of life shape our biology.

In summary, keep these concepts in mind the next time you hear or think that your body must be overweight because it's in your genes or decide that your memory will deteriorate as you age. These areas of study have had a profound impact on the conventional wisdom on aging as well as the idea that our DNA accounts for so many of our biological certainties.

The truth is that your belief has as much of an impact on your reality as any other factor. Are your beliefs moving you closer to the life you want or farther away? If you answered farther away, as I once did, take heart! Beliefs, once recognized, can be changed. I'll show you how.

Sexy Little Twists of Belief and Geeky Science

- Dreams often are abandoned due to a lack of belief.
- Beliefs can be conscious or subconscious, empowering or limiting.
- The mind can be a reckless, undisciplined little rascal until you learn to control it.
- Belief can absolutely change your outcome.
- Make sure your RAS is allowing in the good stuff.
- Through proper care, you can improve the function of your brain. Smart is sexy!

Girl Talk (or Journaling Exercises):

What do you think of the placebo effect? Do you have any personal experience with it, and, if so, what was it? To what extent does *belief* influence a person's healing?

Have you ever experienced your RAS at work? What was it that opened your mind to seeing something new? What did you notice that you hadn't noticed before? What is the learning opportunity in this experience?

If, in fact, our brain can repair itself, what implications does this have on our understanding of the aging process? Do you agree that having a healthy, balanced brain can affect your efforts to change your life for the better? If you knew that your actions could impact your brain in a significant way, what would you be willing to do to keep your brain healthy?

If you knew that the cells of your body responded to your environment, what kind of environment would you want your body to experience? What signals would you want your cells to receive, and how could you send those signals? What would you communicate to your cells?

Discuss how you will use the concepts in this chapter to elevate and improve your results and your life. Commit to one small change that you will make in your daily or weekly habits and be prepared to discuss your experience at the next meeting.

Chapter 3

'Fess Up and Kick It to the Curb

"Vincit quae se vincit."
Latin phrase meaning,
"She conquers, who conquers herself."

All right, girls, here's the tough love part of the pep talk. It's time to take an honest look at what's not working in your life. To make this a little more palatable, let's use an analogy. We're going on a rescue mission.

I'll admit right now to an innate desire to be a hero (or heroine). As a kid, I would daydream and create scenarios in my head where someone needed my help and I came to the rescue—like stumbling upon a recent car accident where someone was trapped, and I helped them escape before the car fell over a cliff. Or I was in danger and overcame tremendous obstacles to save myself from the "bad guys." I always wondered if it was rare for a girl to think that way. Movies, books, and television shows tended to give the hero role to men;

women mostly sat around waiting to be rescued. Not that I was opposed to the idea of being rescued by a handsome guy, but the helpless damsel role just didn't completely resonate with me. I know now that I'm not alone in this thinking. I believe that we all want to be the heroine of our own story. We all want to employ our strengths and gifts in the pursuit of something noble, something bigger than ourselves. And that is precisely the journey upon which we are getting ready to embark.

> *"The 'hero's journey' is grounded in mobilizing, nurturing and regularly renewing our most precious resource—energy—in the service of what matters most."*
> **—Jim Loehr**

"Your mission, should you choose to accept it . . . "

Someone is in need of rescue. She's not a helpless captive, but she does need a champion. She is an amazing, vibrant, lovely person, who is full of life and a sheer joy to be around. She's talented and funny. She's so confident and comfortable in her own head, heart, and body that she's perfectly at ease in any situation. She's strong, kind, and so much fun to be around that she lifts the spirits of everyone she comes into contact with. She acknowledges and makes an effort to overcome her weaknesses, and she uses her God-given talents to become her best, authentic self and serve others in a manner that brings profound joy to those who know her.

I know you recognize her already—she's YOU!

You, before you let life wear you down. You, before you put on a layer of tough to protect your soft heart. You, before someone convinced you that you were stupid or ugly or clumsy or selfish. You, before you gave up on your dreams to follow his or to provide for your family or to become a responsible adult. You, before you stopped wasting time on a silly dream. Before you got a real job or got your head out of the clouds. You, before you had your heart stomped on or your innocence stolen or your talents overlooked. You, before you battled a sickness or miscarried a baby or watched a loved one die. You, before the accident or the attack.

Sometime, long before all that, you were a bundle of hope and joy with bright eyes and big dreams. And we're going to get you back.

You see, beneath the sadness, anger, frustration, and disappointment, you're still in there. Beneath that layer of disillusionment, the resignation that "what I have should be enough," is that hopeful, bright-eyed girl. The one that hasn't quite given up on the idea of asking a little more out of life.

And you still *know* her. She's the one that brings a tear to your eye when you see someone giving their whole self over to an activity, like singing or dancing or making a sale or designing a bridge or helping someone who could use a hand. She's that twinge of envy you feel when you learn of someone's success—an amazing job, a trip of a lifetime, a new home, a blissful marriage. She's that voice that asks, "Is this all there is?"

Incidentally, she's the one that made you pick up this book.

She's been trapped for quite a while beneath layers of life experiences that didn't pan out the way she had hoped. Where the happiness, successes, and joys of your life help pull her to the surface, your fears, sorrows, and disillusionments are like nets and chains that serve to hold her down, keep her quiet, and erase her dreams.

But it doesn't have to be that way. We can get her back. And by "we," I mean mostly you! I'm here to give you hope, to convince you that it can be done, and to give you some weapons to help you on your journey. But only you can be the "boots on the ground." Only you can be the heroine in your own story. And let me tell you, you've got what it takes!

I won't lie to you. Like any other rescue mission, odds are good it won't be easy. In fact, it may just be downright difficult, a path fraught with hard work, discomfort, setbacks, and even a bit of danger. A mission like this one is not for the faint of heart. But consider, for a moment, that it's a life you're saving. Consider, for a moment, that it's a loved one who is trapped, whose gifts are being squandered, and whose passion for life is slowly ebbing away while we stand and watch and shake our heads in pity at the sadness of it all.

Well, not me. I say, "Let's DO SOMETHING!" Rather than be content to stand by watching this travesty, let's step forward and put a stop to it! If you can't muster the courage to do it for your current self, do it for your eight-year-old self.

Even on her worst days, your eight-year-old self still knows that there is more. She knows that life is not about hiding and suppressing her gifts and her passions, but about celebrating and sharing them and using them to serve others. She knows she's not here to numb her mind and heart to those gifts and passions. What would be the point?

So for this chapter, I'll be your drill sergeant during basic training. And like basic training, it may feel as if you're being broken down. It may feel as if I'm adding insult to your injuries, as if I just don't understand the pain you're going through. Take heart, strong one!

The truth is we need to study and overcome some crap before we launch our rescue mission. We review our previous failed attempts so we know what didn't work and don't keep trying the same thing over again. We study the terrain so we know the best way to go in. And we learn our captor's weaknesses so we can make plans to overcome them. Courage, girls! We'll get through!

Our Previous Failed Attempts–
Things That Seemed Like a Good Idea at the Time

You may be wondering why we would look at our previous failures in a book that's all about moving on. Let's just be clear on this one right up front: moving on to a better, brighter future requires an honest, healthy assessment of the past and present. We cannot ignore our past, but we don't have to dwell in it either. In fact, it is the very act of trying to ignore or suppress our past that keeps us stuck in it. Avoiding the truth consumes great effort and energy. Facing the truth frees it up. Keep in mind, however, that truth without compassion is just mean, so we're going to go at the truth with a healthy dose of compassion and understanding.

I'm proposing three specific steps to the process of moving on in a healthy, successful way. They include full disclosure, forgiving yourself, and realizing the noble purpose of your failures, especially your most embarrassing and painful ones.

Full Disclosure

I want you to take a good, hard look at what's not working in your life. Take some time with the questions in this section. Write down your answers in your

Sexy Little Twist journal. And be honest. No one else has to see what you've written; you can burn the pages later. And as you consider these questions, make sure that you're answering from your own heart. Be careful not to answer the questions the way anyone else (your spouse, your parents, your boss, your employees, your pastor, your children, your friends, or other assorted relatives) would expect you to answer. This doesn't mean that those people in your life aren't amazing, enlightened, and joyful people who are so supportive that they could really help you get to the bottom of it. Maybe they are, maybe they aren't. But what they are not is YOU. You came into this world as a whole being, in and of yourself. Just as all others do, you have a purpose to fulfill, and you (and you alone) know what your purpose is. And if you mentally just disagreed with me, I'm here to tell you that you're wrong. Flat-out wrong. The answers are inside of you waiting to be rediscovered. Just trust me for now.

So take some time to answer these questions about what's currently not working in your life.

Are you passionate about the work you're doing to earn a living? Are you regularly utilizing your gifts and strengths in your job or career? Do you feel that something is missing in your work, or that there is a job or career out there that would better match your passions and gifts? (Notice that I don't ask about a "skills" match in this question. Skills can be learned; passions are connected to your soul's deepest calling.) Are you generally excited to get out of bed to go to work? Or do you hit the snooze button numerous times, get up in time to rush through your morning routine, and screech to a halt at your desk just before your boss walks by on her way to the coffee machine? Does your work life allow enough free time for you to rejuvenate regularly?

Are your finances in order? Do you pay the minimum payment on your credit cards each month? Are you completely tapped out in the last few days before you get your next paycheck? Do you have enough in your checking account to cover repairs to your car or washing machine if it's suddenly necessary? Are you putting anything aside for retirement, or your kids' college tuition, or that new home you're wanting? If you're tempted to throw this book in the garbage right now, please remember that this is the tough love part of the pep talk. This is you being honest with you. No one else can or should be the judge. For example, many people, myself included, think their kids would be better served by being encouraged to qualify for scholarships and earn the bulk of their own college expenses themselves. Like me, saving for your kids' college tuition might not top the list of priorities. Remember that you're doing this to get an honest assessment of where YOU think and feel that you are, financially speaking.

Do you enjoy healthy relationships with the people in your life? Is your home environment peaceful and built on love, respect, and mutual admiration? How healthy is your marriage? Do you have friends who challenge and lift you, or do they bring you down? How about family connections? Are you comfortable with your current relationship with your parents and siblings? Are your interactions with your coworkers, boss, and/or employees based on respect and a shared desire to accomplish goals? How about casual acquaintances—are you on friendly terms with the people in your community who serve you at the grocery store or dry cleaners?

How is your health? Are you heavier than you're comfortable with? Do you have enough energy to make it through the day? Do you get sick often? Are you ignoring a health issue or a potential one? Are you burying your head in the sand about an aspect of your health that needs attention? Are you active or sedentary? Do you spend any time outdoors, in nature? Do you have the strength, energy, and endurance to enjoy your free time?

Do you have any hobbies that bring you joy when you engage in them? Have you let go of some activity that you used to love because you no longer have time, or you feel bad spending time doing it, or think you're too old, or you don't have the energy? Do you feel envy when you hear of someone doing something fun or challenging or thrilling? What activity is that? Are you taking the vacations that you dream of? Are you making plans so that you can take them in the future?

Are you comfortable and at peace with your level of spiritual development? Do you attend a church service as much as you would like to? Do you meditate as much as you want to? Do you know everything you'd like to about your chosen faith? Is it a faith you feel strongly about, one that nurtures your soul?

Do you acknowledge that you have resources that can be used to benefit other people? Are you giving back in your community or within your circle of influence? Are you serving others in some way, sharing what you've been given? Are you satisfied with your level of contribution to your community, your church, your children's school, and the world?

The answers to these questions help you assess what hasn't been working in your life until now. Admittedly, it's not the most thrilling part of making a comeback, but it is critical. Taking an honest look at our past failures is the first step in making sure that we don't repeat them.

Forgive Yourself

Before you get too depressed letting the list you've just made sink in, let's get to the next step in the process, which is forgiving yourself for everything that you've done in the past. We are far too prone to beating ourselves up over our missteps, even those that were only identifiable as mistakes AFTER the event took place. I want you to commit to treating yourself a little more gently in the future.

> *"If you talked to your friends the way you talked to your body, you'd have no friends left."*
> **—Marcia Hutchinson**

Think about this quote in the sense of how you talk to yourself in general, not just to your body. Is it a true statement? I'm betting that it is, because most of us are that way. We feel perfectly at ease berating ourselves in our heads, asking harmful questions such as, "How could you do that?" or "Why do you always screw things up?"

In her book *Feel the Fear and Do It Anyway*, Susan Jeffers calls this our "mental chatter." And it not only makes us feel worse in the present moment, but it also increases the odds that we'll make the same mistake the next time.

So regarding every single note you made from the above list of questions, recognize and appreciate that you did the very best you could with the knowledge and resources that you had at the time.

For the first few years after I moved out of my parents' house, my finances were a disaster. My credit card debt was so high that I often could not afford the minimum payments. I would run out of money long before I got my next paycheck. My son and I regularly ate scrambled eggs and a can of green beans for dinner, because it was all I could afford. Debt collectors constantly hounded me on the phone. Lack of immediate funds had me putting off minor auto repairs until they became major financial problems.

During this time, do you think I was mentally cutting myself a break for the mess I was in? Of course not. Like everyone else, I believed that any self-respecting adult would be berating themselves for the situation I was in. How could a person learn from mistakes if they didn't make themselves feel like crap over making them in the first place?

Unfortunately for me at the time, and for all of us who think this way, this is exactly the opposite of what should happen. Sure, we need to acknowledge that we've made a mistake (face the truth). But to beat ourselves up mentally only serves to keep us stuck. We may not make the same mistake, but we'll darn sure make new ones—maybe even worse ones, like I did. Asking questions like, "Why do I always screw things up?" only had me subconsciously screwing up in new and creative ways.

So, I want you to look at your list of what's not working in your life and then, with all the kindness you can muster, acknowledge that you did the best you could at the time. Forgive yourself. This is really difficult to do, and it doesn't come naturally, so keep at it.

If this is too much of a stretch because you're just getting started, think of someone in your life who accepted you just as you are. It might have been a grandparent, or a teacher, or a friend, or a pastor. If you can't think of anyone in your life who was or is that open and accepting, use me. Better yet, use a spiritual guide from your particular faith—God, Jesus, the Dalai Lama, Mohammad, Buddha, etc. Pretend that person (or being) is sitting with you now. What would they think of you mentally abusing yourself? If you're using me as an example, I can assure you that no matter how big the mistake, I want you to stop beating yourself up. You are forgiven for whatever you did in the past. By keeping yourself stuck in past mistakes, you only rob yourself, and the rest of the world, of your best, brightest self. You cannot be in a position to serve others while you're holding a grudge against yourself. Let it go. Forgive you.

Learn from Them

With forgiveness comes the ability to truly learn from our past failures. Again, using the list you've made, spend a few minutes contemplating each item with the following question:

"What is the learning opportunity in this experience?"

The importance of this step cannot be overstated. This is where real growth occurs in your journey. Notice the difference in the approach of this question, compared to the one I always asked myself:

"Why do I keep screwing up?"

This latter question serves to keep me mired in the past, continually rehashing and replaying the weaknesses that prompted the failure in the first place. The former question, the one that takes us beyond wallowing in the past, is the one we want to carry with us every day and into every situation that didn't go as we had hoped. By asking, "What is the learning opportunity in this experience?" we move out of our past and look toward a brighter, happier future.

So take an honest look at where you are now, acknowledge that you did the best you could at the time, and ask yourself what you can learn from your past mistakes. Only by doing this can we make sense of our mistakes. Wouldn't it be great to view our mistakes as having a noble purpose in our lives? In fact, in asking and answering this question, you can and will begin to develop a true appreciation for your mistakes. Will you still make mistakes? Yes. I can assure you that not all of my financial endeavors are successful. But by learning from my earlier financial mishaps, I am now far beyond where I was back then. I can now face my financial situation, knowing that my credit score is in the 800s and being hounded by debt collectors is a thing of the past. If one called me now, I'd honestly be able to tell them they had the wrong number.

Sexy Little Twists of Heroism and Forgiveness:

- Moving on requires an honest, healthy assessment of where we are.
- Mentally beating ourselves up for mistakes only causes repetition of them.
- Face the truth, and then forgive; you did your best at the time.

- Ask yourself, "What's the learning opportunity?" in every experience.
- Rescue yourself; no one else is coming.

Girl Talk (or Journaling Exercises):

What is an area of your life that is not working for you? How would you like it to be different?

What's one mistake that you made in your past that contributed to your current situation? What factors at the time contributed to your decision?

Are you willing to forgive yourself for it? Say it out loud. "I forgive myself for …"

What is the learning opportunity in this experience?

How can you turn it into a noble purpose for your future?

Discuss how you will use the concepts in this chapter to elevate and improve your results and your life. Commit to one small change that you will make in your daily or weekly habits and be prepared to discuss your experience at the next meeting.

Chapter 4

Passion Assassin–the Silent Party Pooper

"Whose party punch have you been drinking?
And how's that tasting?"
—Danne Reed

I remember a scare in the late seventies when a cult leader convinced his followers to drink Flavor Aid™ laced with cyanide. The idea that anyone would willingly pick up the load of garbage that guy was laying down and adopt a belief so contrary to their own nature, so detrimental to the primal desire to *live*, was shocking, to say the least.

But through this extreme example, we can learn something useful. While we create many of our passion assassins in our own mind, another good percentage of them are adopted from others we encounter and interact with throughout our lives. Even well-meaning adults—parents, teachers, Girl Scout leaders, youth group ministers, friends, coworkers, bosses, etc.—have passion assassins of their own, and often pass those on to others.

As you work through the exercises in this chapter, hold the question in the back of your mind, "Whose party punch am I drinking?" Whose beliefs have you adopted that are even now getting in the way of the joyful, passionate life you desire and deserve? It's time to let go of other people's beliefs (OPBs) and create and nurture your own more inspiring, more empowering ones. Dump that stagnant, watery concoction down the drain and mix your own, with some fresh ingredients and a splash of your own passion! It all starts with identifying what's in your glass right now.

We discussed the importance of belief in Chapter 2, but here we need to take this concept a step further. If you are in your thirties or beyond and you are feeling as if you have not yet achieved success in a certain area or areas of your life (career, financial, relationships, personal, spiritual, etc.), then you most likely have one or more passion assassins or limiting beliefs. The things that aren't working to your satisfaction in your life right now are likely the direct result of the passion assassins that you carry. Unless you take steps to eradicate them as you try to move beyond your mistakes into a new area of growth, success, and happiness, these passion assassins will creep up and sabotage your progress.

As I mentioned in Chapter 2, passion assassins can be conscious, meaning we're well aware of the thought (though we may not identify it as a passion assassin); or subconscious, meaning that we're operating under them without being fully aware we're doing so. And since we can't very well get rid of beliefs we're not fully aware of, let's talk about some ways to *identify* your passion assassins.

Generalizations, Clichés, and "Collective Assumptions"

What do you know to be true about being successful in any area of your life? When you think about trying to accomplish something that you haven't before (whether it's building a new home, getting started in a new career, having a happy, healthy marriage, or competing in a triathlon), what comes to mind?

Do you recall sayings or clichés you heard about getting wealthy or learning something new? All of us grew up hearing these sayings. Maybe we paid attention, maybe we didn't. But I'll bet some of them took, regardless of whether or not you realized it.

When I decided to show up Fashionably Late to my own life, I realized that I wanted to eliminate as many passion assassins as I could. I began the process of uncovering my passion assassins by searching for "cliché examples." I perused lists of clichés on the Internet in order to find any that resonated with me and perhaps uncover passion assassins that I didn't realize I had. A cliché is a perfect example of a "collective assumption." It's been used so many times that it's become ingrained in the way we think, speak, and act. While they originally were coined and repeated by often well-meaning parents, to help us avoid hurt and disappointment or to teach us a valuable lesson, clichés are not necessarily empowering. When used in a negative way, they can be quite the opposite. Here are some examples that resonated with me, and perhaps you'll identify with them as well:

"The acorn doesn't fall far from the tree."

The takeaway: Even though they may try, people end up just like their parents.

"Always a bridesmaid, never the bride."

The takeaway: Your girlfriends adore you, but don't expect a man to. In a movie of your own life, you'd be the best supporting actress, never the leading lady.

"Another day, another dollar."

The takeaway: Life is a grind. We're at the mercy of those who pay us to work, day in and day out.

"Better safe than sorry."

The takeaway: Don't take risks.

"The bigger they are, the harder they fall."

The takeaway: Probably originally meant to encourage those who would try to compete with the successful (think David and Goliath), this one is a double-edged sword—don't get too successful or someone will topple *you*.

"A bird in the hand is worth two in the bush."

The takeaway: Don't try for more; you will likely lose what you have.

"Don't bite off more than you can chew."

The takeaway: Don't take big risks; you'll choke.

"You can't have your cake and eat it, too."

The takeaway: Be satisfied with not having everything you want.

"You can't squeeze blood out of a turnip."

The takeaway: Some things are impossible; don't even try.

"You can't teach an old dog new tricks."

The takeaway: We can do less as we get older.

"Champagne taste on a beer budget."

The takeaway: Don't wish for things you can't afford.

"Damned if you do, damned if you don't."

The takeaway: You'll lose no matter what you do.

"Dog eat dog."

The takeaway: Everyone is out to beat you down.

"Filthy rich." Or "Money hungry."

The takeaway: People have to play dirty in order to obtain large amounts of money. People who pursue wealth are greedy and selfish.

"You'd lose your head if it wasn't attached."

The takeaway: You're hopelessly scatterbrained.

"If you don't have anything nice to say, don't say anything at all."

The takeaway: Another one with a double edge. Most likely originally meant to keep people from saying mean things to each other, this one also is commonly used to keep people from voicing an opposing opinion.

"A jack of all trades and master of none."

The takeaway: On the positive side, this is meant to keep people from spreading themselves too thin. On the negative side, the message is that you can be successful in only one area.

"Keep your nose to the grindstone."

The takeaway: Being successful sounds downright painful, doesn't it?

"A leopard can't change its spots."

The takeaway: People are unable to change.

"Life's a bitch."

The takeaway: Life's a bitch. 'Nough said.

"Luck of the draw."

The takeaway: We can't change our luck.

"We're not made of money." Or "Money doesn't grow on trees."

The takeaway: Only people who are born into money ever have money. We're not rich and never will be.

"Money can't buy you happiness."

The takeaway: Having money isn't a worthy pursuit since it won't change anything anyway.

"Money is the root of all evil."

The takeaway: Money is the root of all evil. The original verse from the Bible tells us that the *worship* of money is the root of all evil. Its meaning has been hijacked by those who would discourage the pursuit of money, period.

"Sometimes you're the hydrant, sometimes you're the dog," or

"Sometimes you're the windshield, sometimes you're the bug."

The takeaway: While I appreciate these two sayings for sheer comedic factor alone, the message is that in all of life's interactions, there's only the victor or the victim.

"That's the way the cookie crumbles" (or the ball bounces).

The takeaway: There's nothing you can do to change the situation.

"Waiting for the other shoe to drop."

The takeaway: Something bad is about to happen.

"When it rains, it pours."

The takeaway: When something bad happens, more bad things happen next.

If you find yourself nodding your head or identifying with any of these statements, you probably have an associated passion assassin. So, one way to identify your passion assassins is to check out lists of clichés or familiar sayings and see which ones ring true for you. Again, many if not most of these familiar sayings can be very helpful and can contribute to a healthy belief system.

The question you'll want to ask yourself is, "Does this statement make me feel empowered or disempowered?" If you get a negative feeling, try playing with the phrase in order to turn it into something more powerful for you.

Using the example of "money is the root of all evil," try thinking "money is the root of all giving" or "money is the root of all weekend spa retreats." Or turn the example of "champagne taste on a beer budget" into "champagne tastes spectacular on a beer budget." Or try "money can't buy happiness, but I'm sure my son's college will take it anyway"; or "money can't buy you happiness, but it'll sure pay for that beach house."

The idea is to turn the statement into a positive one, preferably with humor so it will stick in your brain. Then, anytime you hear or think the original cliché, replace it with your new and improved version. Over time, you'll look forward to hearing the old version, because you'll get a chuckle out of it.

Specific Goal Obstacles

Another way to uncover passion assassins is to think of a specific goal that you would like to achieve, and then sit quietly and be aware of the thoughts that come to your mind as you contemplate achieving that goal. Try the following exercise.

At the top of a fresh page in your journal, write down one major goal that you would love to achieve. Choose a goal that really seems like a stretch for you right now, but one that you would dearly LOVE to accomplish.

Some suggestions:

- Write and publish a bestselling book.
- Open my own restaurant.
- Become a world-famous singer.
- Build my dream home.
- Take a six-month sabbatical and travel the world.
- Have enough money invested to live off the dividends.

Or choose any other goal that excites you. Write it down at the top of the page.

Now sit quietly for a few moments and think about achieving that goal. You see, there's a reason you haven't already achieved it. You've established that it's something that you're passionate about, so why don't you have it in your life right now?

Answer the following questions as you think about your goal (adapted from Anisa Aven's, CEO of CreataVision Enterprises, questions on her website CreataVision.com):

1. What might I lose if I achieve this goal? What problems will it cause? How will it negatively impact me or others?
2. What can't be changed that prevents me from reaching this goal? What are some reasons this goal is impossible to achieve? What causes things to stay the way they are now?
3. There's a part of me that doesn't want to achieve this goal because . . .
4. What's my personal deficiency or dysfunction that prevents me from achieving this goal? What makes me incapable of achieving it?
5. What have I done, or not done, that makes me unworthy of getting what I want? I don't deserve to have what I want because . . .
6. What makes fulfillment of my goal wrong or inappropriate? It's wrong to want to be different because . . .

The answers to these questions will go a long way toward helping you identify passion assassins, at least in regard to achieving your particular goal. You could do this exercise with each and every goal that you have (more on goal setting in Chapter 11). And if you did this with each of your goals, you likely would begin to see patterns emerge. The same passion assassins likely are plaguing you in several different areas of your life.

For example, I might set a goal to start a new career and another to learn to play the piano. An underlying belief that we lose our ability to learn new things as we get older ("you can't teach an old dog new tricks") will certainly hinder me in both pursuits.

Another example might be a goal to build my dream home and another to take a sabbatical and travel the world. If I have a belief that only people born into money will ever be really wealthy, and I also hold the belief that you have to be wealthy to do these things, then I'll likely struggle to achieve either goal.

Meaning Derived from Our Failures

Take a look at the notes you made at the beginning of this chapter on what's currently not working in your life. Just pick one area or even one statement you made in any of the areas. It might be that you aren't currently passionate about your work, or you're not happy with your weight. Just choose one.

Got it?

As you consider that "failure", what comes to mind? Can you think of reasons why you're in that situation? Do you have negative thoughts about it and chastise yourself for even struggling with it? Do you justify or rationalize why it is so? Do you blame someone, or something, or even your own deficiencies?

Using the example of not being happy with your weight, do you think that you're overweight because it's genetic? Your parents or siblings are overweight, so you can't control it? Or were you taught bad eating habits as a child? Or do your children or spouse or job monopolize your time so you can't squeeze a workout into your day? Anything that comes to mind here should be examined as a passion assassin.

In the example of not being passionate about your job, do you think that work is work and play is play, and that the two don't mix? Do you think that you need to make a living, so waiting around for a job you enjoy isn't practical? Or perhaps you believe that you're not smart enough, young enough, or financially secure enough for the job you really want?

Keep in mind that these questions are not intended to make you feel bad or to have you beating up on yourself. I'm quite sure you do enough of that already. The goal of asking the questions is to *really* examine the stories you tell yourself in order to discover where you have beliefs that are limiting your success. And as in the exercise above, if you take the time to go through each of the failures you listed, you will see belief patterns emerge.

One other quick exercise for uncovering passion assassins is to force yourself, for a brief moment, to recall your most embarrassing, most gut-wrenching moments. The things you hear in your head as you think about those mortifying moments in time will give you strong indications of your beliefs about yourself.

Some years ago, I was asked to produce a training video for a division of the corporation where I worked. What a great opportunity to share my knowledge on a larger scale, right? Unfortunately, no. When the producer turned the camera on me, I took a deep breath . . . and froze. And I don't just mean the brief stutter and quick recovery kind of freeze. I mean dry mouth, sweaty palms, deer-in-the-headlights, forgot-my-own-name panic. After an hour or so, the frustrated producer finally gave up and later managed to piece together a few seconds of usable video in which I *didn't* look like a complete idiot.

A few years later, my second experience with being on camera went quite similarly and resulted in a surprise "outtakes" video at a meeting, which had over a hundred of my colleagues rolling on the floor with laughter. I sat with my head in my hands, wishing for a black hole to swallow me. My secret was out. I was horrible at something, and now everyone knew it. Perhaps most mortifying of all, the film even captured me looking at my hand after wiping my nose! I know . . . I'm so sophisticated and glamorous.

As I reflected on this incident later, I realized that I was holding a belief that I had to be perfect in order to be respected. In fact, the immediate outcome of that incident was that the atmosphere in that meeting became more relaxed and fun. The long-term result was that my colleagues were far more comfortable approaching me, because they felt a deeper connection with me. I guess lots of people check out their own snot.

Seriously, we all have our weaknesses. Though it wasn't my idea to "out" one of mine, the outcome was a more real, authentic working relationship with my colleagues.

For now, your job is to become consciously aware that you have these passion assassins. Begin taking notes when these thoughts come up so you can eradicate them. We'll talk about how to eliminate them in Chapter 12.

Sexy Little Twists of Awareness

- Dump OPBs down the drain and drink your own party punch.
- Identify your passion assassins so you can kill them first.
- Clichés that resonate give us clues to our passion assassins.
- Passion assassins often sneak up on us when we contemplate achieving big goals.

Girl Talk (or Journaling Exercises):

What is an area of your life that is currently not working for you? Do you have strong beliefs about why it's not working; if so, what are they?

Did any of the clichés listed above ring a bell? Where did you first hear or read the cliché? Was it from a parent or teacher? What message do you think they were trying to convey? What message are you continuing to tell yourself now that doesn't serve you?

Share one of your big goals with the group. What do you imagine you will have to give up in order to achieve the goal?

If you're willing, share an embarrassing experience with the group. What did you tell yourself at the time it happened? What do you tell yourself about the incident now?

Pick a cliché—either from the list above or one of your own—and create a new and improved version. Share it with the group.

Discuss how you will use the concepts in this chapter to elevate and improve your results and your life. Commit to one small change that you will make in your daily or weekly habits and be prepared to discuss your experience at the next meeting.

Part II
Stirring Things Up

"The most courageous act is still to think for yourself. Aloud."
—**Coco Chanel**

Chapter 5

The Life of the Party
(That's You, by the Way)!

*"Everything that happens to you is a reflection of what you believe
about yourself. We cannot outperform our level of self-esteem. We
cannot draw to ourselves more than we think we are worth."*

—Iyanla Vanzant

Your Captor's Weakness—When the Enemy Is You

The intriguing aspect of the rescue mission analogy is that while you
can easily see that you are the captive, it may be a little more difficult
to realize (but it is no less true) that you are also the captor!

Suppressing or hiding our true nature is the work of a low self-esteem. This
isn't a blanket statement that's meant to pass judgment on your whole being. It's
entirely possible that you have quite high self-esteem in the area of work and low

self-esteem when it comes to parenting or relationships. Or the reverse could be true. The point is, you may be quite confident in some areas of your life, but feel completely inept in others.

We have two options regarding self-esteem. We can either remain unconscious of it working within us, or we can acknowledge it as the major force that it is and seek to improve it. Either way, it's at work inside of us, every moment, every day. High or low, healthy or not, our self-esteem is a constant factor in our thoughts and feelings, choices and actions.

The essence of self-esteem, according to Nathaniel Branden, a recognized authority on the topic, is to trust one's mind and to know that one is worthy of happiness. And the true power of self-esteem lies in not merely feeling and judging that we are worthy of happiness, but in the motivation and behavior that it inspires.

Self-esteem is more than a characteristic that someone is either raised from childhood to possess in adulthood, or not. Since self-esteem is at the same time a cause and an effect, it is a part of our self that can be honed and nurtured, even if we didn't acquire the gift as we were growing up. Certainly children whose self-esteem is encouraged and nurtured by the adults in their lives may have a head start over those children whose self-esteem is not nurtured; but all of us, no matter what age, can nurture and improve our own self-esteem. In fact, we're the only ones who can take the job and have any hope of success.

Understanding this point is critical to living your life with a Sexy Little Twist. If you have passion assassins about what you can achieve or a low self-esteem regarding what you deserve, then you'll tend to sabotage your own progress. When you answered the questions in Chapter 3 about what's not currently working in your life, you acknowledged that there is something better out there than what you have now. Your true, authentic self recognizes that it's being cheated out of the best that life has to offer. This indicates that your self-esteem could use some nurturing in this area. If you have a belief that you're not worthy of great wealth, that living paycheck-to-paycheck is all you deserve, then you will subtly sabotage your success if your results begin to show otherwise. If your level of success in finances doesn't feel appropriate to you, given what you believe about yourself, then you will subconsciously take steps to knock yourself back in this area.

An example: When I was in the midst of my financial woes early in my adulthood, I would occasionally get a break through a raise at work or an unexpected tax refund. Because I carried a belief that I would always struggle financially, I would squander those financial opportunities by spending the bulk of it, rather than using it to pay down debt.

Some might read this and think that it was a lack of self-control rather than a subconscious need to stay in my comfort zone of "financially struggling." But I had plenty of self-control in other areas of my life. I was a dedicated employee and devoted single mother. I had plenty of opportunities to lose self-control in those areas, but I did not. Why? Simply because of a limiting belief that I was not "cut out" for wealth. Oh sure, I pined for wealth and daydreamed about what it would be like to have it; but when I had opportunities to create real wealth (improve my net worth), I chose not to see or treat them that way. And so I stayed stuck for quite a while.

As with passion assassins, a low self-esteem in one area can spill over into other areas of life. I know a woman who was at the pinnacle of her career and was getting ready to close the business deal of a lifetime. It would have skyrocketed her success and all but secured her and her family's financial future. But as the signing of the deal got closer, her drinking got worse and worse. With the final deal closing only days away, her home life fell apart, her husband took their children and left her, and she was left with no option but to check herself into a rehab center. Coincidental timing? I don't believe so. I believe that while she was confident enough in her ability to perform in her career, she had a low self-esteem about her deservingness of such a level of success. Being that successful was too far outside of her comfort zone, and she took steps, however unconsciously, to pull herself back to where she thought she belonged.

So, as with passion assassins, we must address the underlying self-esteem that causes us to take actions, or to *not* take actions. If our self-esteem is high, we'll have feelings and think thoughts and take actions that bring us closer to what we truly desire. If our self-esteem is low, we'll have feelings and think thoughts and take actions that pull us away from our heart's desires and our soul's callings.

Ironically, those very actions, produced by our self-esteem, can generate momentum in one direction or the other, as long as we're conscious of our self-esteem at work in us.

Let me explain. If we make a conscious attempt to raise our self-esteem and we take action toward any goal, then we'll probably begin to feel uncomfortable. You know that squirmy feeling that something's just not right? If we're aware that the discomfort is simply lingering residue, what I like to call "leftovers" of a low self-esteem, then we can overcome the tendency to step back into our old comfort zone. Upon overcoming that tendency toward a knee-jerk reaction to go back to where we were before, our self-esteem actually gets a boost at this point in our journey. We grow, if just a little, in our self-respect and self-trust. When this simple but profound process is repeated over and over again, self-esteem is improved exponentially.

For example, consider a person who wants to lose twenty pounds. They start out the first morning by getting up early and exercising before work. Already, they are outside of their fitness comfort zone. A low fitness self-esteem will have them seeking to replace all of the calories they burned that morning, and then some, at lunch or sooner. If they're aware of this tendency and choose to step firmly in the direction of greater fitness by eating a healthy meal at lunch, then their fitness self-esteem gets a boost. When this cycle is repeated enough times, self-esteem is raised ever higher; it is bolstered by the self-respect, self-trust, and self-awareness that are occurring, not to mention the physical evidence of a narrowing waistline.

In contrast, if the person chooses to eat an unhealthy meal at lunch after exercising in the morning, their fitness self-esteem takes a hit. They think to themselves things like, "I knew you couldn't do it. You're hopeless. You can't be trusted to follow through on the smallest commitment." When this cycle is repeated enough times, self-esteem is lowered. The person loses self-respect and self-trust.

Though my focus in this book is not to delve deeply into the topic of self-esteem, it is a critical component to living your life with a Sexy Little Twist. Therefore, I want to share with you an overview of what makes up healthy self-esteem, as relayed by Nathaniel Branden in his book *The Six Pillars of Self-Esteem*.

I highly recommend reading this book, and any others you can get your hands on, if you feel that an unhealthy self-esteem is hindering your progress. It really is a foundational issue that cannot be overlooked if you want to move into a new phase of life.

What Does Self-Esteem Look Like?

In action, high self-esteem manifests itself through the following:

Rationality and realism—The base of self-esteem is a respect for facts; a recognition that what is, is; what is not, is not. Consider the exercises you completed in Chapter 3, in which you took an honest look at what's not working in your life. Doing that exercise, though it might have been uncomfortable, connected you with what's real—your current reality. Interestingly, studies prove that those with low self-esteem tend to underestimate or overestimate their abilities; those with high self-esteem tend to assess their abilities realistically. Think about that for a minute. A low self-esteem can cause you to believe you are either far worse off than you are or far better off than you are. With a high self-esteem, you see yourself as you really are.

Intuitiveness—A mind that trusts itself is more likely to rely on and manage intuition effectively by appropriately testing the facts. A mind that doesn't trust itself will not lean on intuition. A person with high self-esteem will be more likely to pay attention to gut feelings, and, thus, be more likely to act on those intuitions. In an ever-expanding cycle, they often will be rewarded for those actions, further proving that they should continue to trust their gut feelings.

Creativity—This one is closely related to intuition. People with high self-esteem tend to value the productions of their mind. They learn from and are inspired by others, but they value their own thoughts and insights. Those with low self-esteem tend to discount the productions of their own mind. They may have worthwhile ideas, but they don't value them, don't treat them as potentially important, and rarely act on them.

Flexibility and the ability to manage change—A mind that trusts itself is able to respond quickly to novelty, because it is open to seeing it. In contrast, clinging to the past in the face of new and changing circumstances is a product of insecurity, a lack of self-trust. You've made it this far in a book all about transforming yourself through small changes, so you obviously have not set out to cling to your past.

Willingness to admit (and correct) mistakes—Healthy self-esteem is not ashamed to say "I was wrong" when the occasion calls for it. Denial and defensiveness are characteristics of insecurity, guilt, feelings of inadequacy, and shame. It's a low self-esteem that experiences a simple admission of error as humiliation and even self-damnation. I can personally vouch for this one, as it is SO much easier now to apologize for my mistakes than it used to be. It used to feel as if apologizing for anything meant admitting that I was defective as a person, that I was *less than* the person to whom I was apologizing. As my self-esteem has improved, I've seen time and again (I make loads of mistakes) that admitting I was wrong about something actually makes me *more than* the person I was before I acknowledged the error.

Benevolence and cooperativeness—Empathy and compassion are far more likely to be found in a person with high self-esteem, since our relationship with others tends to mirror and reflect our relationship with ourselves. The world is a mirror, right? We dislike ourselves; we tend to dislike others. We like who we are; we tend to appreciate who others are. This one is as simple as math—one plus one equals two. It's one of the hardest ones to see, though. We often don't connect the dots between how we're feeling about others and how we're feeling about ourselves. But the link is there. Improving your self-esteem and learning to adore yourself will open your eyes to a whole new world full of adorable people. Seriously, you'll run into them everywhere.

As you head down the path toward a higher self-esteem, just keep in mind that the challenge is to raise your level of awareness in the face of powerful emotional resistance. You'll have to challenge the idea that your interests are best served by blindness. This can be tough, because often we feel that our lack of awareness is the only thing that makes life bearable. Our reward for holding this belief is that we don't have to take any risks. This is fear, not confidence. This is escaping the scariness of life, not living it. This is safety, not creativity. And in our relationships with others, it is a desire to be forgiven, accepted, and taken care of, rather than a chance to experience real connections.

Here is an exercise to get you started. Take out your Sexy Little Twist journal, set a timer for ten minutes, and finish the following sentences with as many ideas as you can think of. Don't overthink; just write whatever comes to mind without editing as you go. The goal is to get as many items as you can on paper.

1. If I were to trust my gut feelings, my intuition, just a little bit more, I would . . .
2. If I were to value my own creative ideas just a bit more, I would . . .
3. If I were to become just a little more open to change, I would . . .
4. If I were just a bit more willing to admit to my mistakes, I would . . .
5. If I were just a bit more compassionate with others, I would . . .

Do this exercise every day for a week and see how, without even taking any deliberate action, it will change your mindset. You will find yourself acting in ways that support what you've written. You may get enough benefit from this that you choose to do it every day. It's a beautiful way of getting in touch with yourself, with your true inner being.

Living your life with a Sexy Little Twist requires a higher level of self-awareness, self-respect, and self-trust. Luckily, in addition to exercises such as the one above, a healthy self-esteem can be nurtured and cultivated through the following practices:

Living Consciously—We'll talk more about Living Consciously in Chapter 10; but for now, just know that Living Consciously and mindfully is the quickest path to high self-esteem. To paraphrase Braden, we establish a sense of the kind of person we are through the thousands of choices we make between thinking and non-thinking, being responsible toward reality or evading it. We rarely remember these choices consciously, but deep in our psyche they're added up. The sum is that experience we call *self-esteem*. Living Consciously means that we make a concerted effort to be aware of our choices, purposes, values, and goals (to the best of our ability); and that the actions we take are in line with what we see and know.

Self-acceptance—Self-acceptance is a refusal to be in an adversarial relationship with yourself. To be on your own side. It is you saying, "I choose to value myself and to treat myself with respect." It is you saying, without apology, "I think what I think, feel what I feel, want what I want, have done what I've done, and am what I am." Like the exercise in Chapter 3, it is your willingness to experience rather than disown whatever may be your reality at a particular moment. Self-acceptance is a realization that denying reality only serves to keep us stuck.

Self-responsibility—This is another area that we'll cover in more depth in a later chapter. But briefly, self-responsibility includes the knowledge that you are responsible for:

- The achievement of your desires.
- Your choices and actions.
- The level of consciousness you bring to your work and relationships.
- Your behavior with other people—coworkers, clients, associates, customers, spouses, partners, children, and friends.
- How you prioritize your time.
- The quality of your communications.
- Your personal happiness.
- Accepting or choosing the values by which you live.
- Raising your self-esteem.

This list can be boiled down to three things that you're ultimately responsible for—your thoughts, your feelings, and your actions.

Self-assertiveness—This means honoring your wants, needs, and values and then expressing them appropriately. The opposite of self-assertiveness is a timid surrender of the real you—hiding who you truly are in order to avoid confrontation, to please or manipulate someone, or simply to fit in. Self-assertiveness is a willingness to stand up for yourself, to be who you are openly, and to treat yourself with respect in all your interactions with others. It's a refusal to fake it in order to be liked. This is living authentically, using your innermost convictions as a guide for your life. Holding values is one thing, but standing by them as we "show up" in the world is true self-assertiveness. This is you saying,

"My life is mine alone, and I'm not here to live up to someone else's expectations." Without this, we're spectators to our lives, not participants.

This characteristic has a lot to do with how we "show up" in our relationships with others. We'll cover this in more depth in Chapter 15, because it is so critical to living life with a Sexy Little Twist. For now, just be aware of that self-assertiveness is:

- Being in an intimate relationship without losing our sense of self.
- Being kind without being self-sacrificing.
- Cooperating with others without betraying our standards and convictions.

Doesn't that sound fabulous?

Living purposefully—We'll also cover living purposefully more in Chapter 8. Briefly, living without purpose is living at the mercy of chance. Remember my story about my career and how I pinged around from one job to another without outlining a strategy of my own? I was taking a reactive, rather than a proactive, stance, relying on external forces to provide opportunities that I either took, or didn't. I was drifting. When I finally learned to live more purposefully, I stopped meandering around and started moving more deliberately in the direction I wanted my life to go.

The essence of living purposefully is to:

- Consciously take responsibility for determining our goals and purpose (more to come on this in Chapters 8 and 11).
- Identify the actions necessary to achieve our goals.
- Monitor our own behavior to make sure it's aligned with our goals.
- Pay attention to our results, to know whether we're headed toward where we want to go.

So, it's not really about the accomplishments, although those are certainly exciting and validating. It's more about the *internal practices* that make those accomplishments possible. That's where self-esteem is improved—through what happens on the inside.

Personal integrity—Integrity is that beautiful place where our behavior coincides with our ideals, beliefs, standards, and convictions. When our behavior matches what we say we value, we have integrity. When we act in ways that conflict with our own good judgment, we lose respect for ourselves. If it becomes a habit, we may eventually stop trusting ourselves altogether. Integrity can be found at the intersection of Words Way and Behavior Boulevard. When we take actions that conflict with our own values, we betray our mind, thinking that our judgment is insignificant and that only the judgment of others matters. But the opposite is true when it comes to building self-esteem—my own judgment is the only one that counts.

If you recognize in any of these concepts an opportunity to improve your self-esteem, then not only is it worthwhile, but it's also absolutely essential to living your life with a *Sexy Little Twist*.

The exercise in this chapter and the others in this book will help you do just that!

Sexy Little Twists of Self-Esteem

- When our self-esteem is high, we'll have feelings, think thoughts, and take actions that bring us closer to our desires.
- When we overcome our knee-jerk tendency to slip back into our comfort zone, our self-esteem gets a boost.
- High self-esteem respects reality, trusts gut feelings, values creative ideas, is open to change, admits mistakes, and is compassionate with self and others.
- Self-esteem is cultivated through conscious living, self-acceptance, personal responsibility, assertiveness, purposeful living, and integrity.

Girl Talk (or Journaling Exercises):

Think of an area of your life where you have relatively high self-esteem. What results have you experienced that provide evidence of your success in this area? What are some contributing factors that you feel have led to a higher self-esteem in this area? Share your thoughts with the group.

Think of an area of your life where you have relatively low self-esteem. What results have you experienced that provide evidence of your "failure"? What are some contributing factors that you feel have led to a lower self-esteem in this area? Share your thoughts with the group.

Have you ever set out to achieve a goal but found yourself sabotaging your own progress? What was the goal and what did you do, or *not* do, that kept you from achieving it? Do you think your self-esteem had an impact on your lack of results? If so, in what ways? What would you choose to do now in order to turn it around?

Do you tend to trust your intuition and value your own creative ideas? If so, share an example of a time when something positive resulted from your intuition and/or creativity. If not, share with the group how you might go about honoring your own ideas in the future.

Share with the group a time when you hid or suppressed your true self for the sake of maintaining a relationship and how you felt when spending time with that person. If it's been resolved, how did that happen? If it's not yet resolved, how might you go about resolving it?

Discuss how you will use the concepts in this chapter to elevate and improve your results and your life. Commit to one small change that you will make in your daily or weekly habits and be prepared to discuss your experience at the next meeting.

Chapter 6

Take Charge! After All, It's Your Party!

*"A woman is like a tea bag—you can't tell
how strong she is until you put her in hot water."*
—Eleanor Roosevelt

I got hit by a guy once. Busted my lip open with a well-placed backhand. It wasn't a random assault, since the guy happened to be my boyfriend of two years and the biological father of my then four-week-old son.

In the two years I had been dating him, I had become more and more concerned about his violent behavior when he drank, which he did often. He would regularly instigate fistfights wherever we went—parties, the bowling alley, a gas station one time, even a wedding reception. Incidentally, you know how in your memory some events get a little fuzzy? *That* one is still crystal clear to me.

Unfortunately, I waited until I was pregnant to really open my eyes to the truth. And then I had the internal conflict of breaking it off and raising a child on my own or trying to work things out with the baby's father. Stay or go; stay or go. You know how it is with these tough life decisions. Being young and stupid didn't help either.

My wake-up call came suddenly and painfully, as wake-up calls sometimes do.

In that moment of shock (*Did he seriously just hit me?*), I envisioned the rest of my life playing out in a series of similar episodes, with him commanding the role of the angry tyrant. Me the timid, pathetic wife. And my son, the sad, abused child.

Basically, clarity punched me in the face.

I said nothing; just stood up and held my arms out for my now-screaming son, whom he was holding in his other arm. He hesitated for a brief second and then handed him to me. I turned and walked away, permanently. Many years later, he's now just a guy I used to know.

While I can think of many instances in my life where I gave my power away, that moment wasn't one of them. That was a moment when I took full responsibility for myself (and for my infant son) and became the owner of my life.

Victim or Owner?

In his book *Reinventing Yourself: How to Become the Person You've Always Wanted to Be*, Steven Chandler states that at any given time in our lives, we are either an owner of our human spirit or we are a victim of circumstances. Specifically, he says:

> The ownership way reinvents you as you go, in an ever-expanding circle of compassion, vision, and courage. The other way (the victim way) shrinks you down. Just as your muscles shrink when they are not moving, so do your heart and soul when you are in your victim mode.

Yikes! Who wants to feel shrunken? A fitting word for an awful state of being. But apparently, we sometimes do, subconsciously at least. Ultimately, whether you are a victim or an owner in any given situation is entirely up to you. It's a choice.

Making the correct choice starts with understanding your power. To many of us, the word *power* can have a negative connotation. We've all known people who see power as a tool to try to control others. Whether through overt physical strength or covert manipulative tactics, it's not an attractive picture. But think of power in the simple definition of having the ability or capacity to act or perform effectively. And think of it as something that you apply to yourself only, not to others, and you'll be on the right track.

Acknowledging that we have power over ourselves, and ONLY over ourselves, is essential to becoming an owner of our lives. Owning our results is essential to achieving anything in life, especially our dreams.

As I mentioned in the previous chapter, when we covered personal responsibility as it pertains to self-esteem, our power is in these three simple areas:

- The thoughts we think.
- The feelings we feel.
- The actions we take.

Ultimately, in any given situation, our power lies solely in how we think, feel, and behave.

Conversely, when we see circumstances, events, and other people as the cause of our thoughts, feelings, and behavior, then we have abdicated our power and have become a victim. While it might be difficult, even painful, to grasp the idea, we *choose* our thoughts, feelings, and behaviors in every moment of every day. We choose to be an owner or a victim.

When we choose to be a victim, we see power as something that's outside of ourselves. Something that others possess over us, but we don't have.

While some of these may come as a surprise, here are a few examples of victim thinking:

"My boss really frustrates me."
"My sister really makes me angry."
"This always happens to me."

"I've tried to improve our marriage, but my spouse just won't change."

"Our house is always such a mess, because my kids won't help out."

"I grew up eating this way, so I've always been overweight."

"I don't have time to do what I want, because I volunteer every week."

"I would be wealthy right now if the stock market hadn't crashed."

"This mess I'm in is all my ex-husband's fault."

And even, "My life was forever ruined when he raped me."

What we are saying in each of these examples is that someone else is responsible for or capable of making us happy, for making us wealthy, for bringing us a sense of peace, and for giving our lives meaning.

Ultimately, *no one* has the ability, or the power, to make us do or feel anything, unless we *give that power to them.* I recently read a piece by Byron Katie, author of *Loving What Is: Four Questions That Can Change Your Life,* in which she described helping a grown man work through the pain of being abused by his father as a small child. Part of his transformation came from acknowledging that he was playing a role in his own victimization by allowing the event (his father's horrendous choices and actions) to get in the way of his current peace.

Are you giving away your power? Or are you *owning* your happiness, your state of mind, and your inner peace? And that's what I mean by *power.* Not the kind that implies control over others with the intent to benefit only yourself. When used in that manner, power rarely brings peace, wealth, or happiness to either party. No, what I'm referring to is the power that you have within you to *own* every aspect of your life. From your emotional state in any given moment, to the kind of car you drive, to where you live, to the kind of work you do.

If you're thinking right now that someone else has the power to dictate any of these examples, it may be true, but only because you have *chosen* to give that power to them. Choice and power are directly connected.

And I'm here to tell you that success can only be achieved through taking 100 percent responsibility for every aspect of your life. You must become an owner rather than a victim. You must accept that the power is all within you, not dependent upon anyone or anything else.

I'll admit to being quite skeptical when I first heard this. How could I be responsible for feeling hurt when someone insulted me or angry when someone took advantage of me?

When I was twelve, I had a crush on a classmate named Mike. My friend and I made plans to meet Mike and one of his friends at a recreation center to play pool one Saturday afternoon. When Mike arrived, his friend took one look at me, made a face like he had just vomited in his own mouth, and then shook his head at Mike. It was clear to me from this exchange that Mike had asked his friend for his opinion of me, and, to put it mildly, I had been found lacking.

At this time in my life, I knew of no other way to process this incident than to feel hurt and ugly.

In my mind, the math was simple:

$$\text{Insult} + \text{Me} = \text{Me feeling hurt}$$

But here's some new math for you!

In his book *The Success Principles*, Jack Canfield shares a formula he learned from Dr. Robert Resnick:

$$E + R = O \text{ (Event + Response = Outcome)}$$

While this formula is simple, it is extremely profound in achieving success in any area of your life. At its simplest, it means that everything you currently have (success or failure, wealth or poverty, health or illness, intimacy or estrangement, joy or frustration) is the direct result of how you've responded to earlier events in your life. If you don't like the outcomes you are currently getting, then there are two basic choices you can make:

1. Respond by blaming (R) the event (E) for your unsatisfactory results (O), or,
2. Change your responses (R) to the events (E)—the way things are—until you get the outcomes (O) you want.

So let's use my example from above. What twelve-year-old Danne did when this event occurred was outwardly pretend that I didn't know what had just happened, while inside I began to question myself. "Am I really that ugly? How many other people realize that I'm ugly? Why the hell didn't someone tell me before?" So my response (R) to the incident (E) was to start, and maintain for a period of time, an inner dialogue that supported the idea that I was disgustingly unattractive.

Now, let's suppose twelve-year-old me had known about E + R = O. Suppose I had known then that I could *choose* my response to anything and everything that happened around me. When Mike's friend made the vomit face (E), I might have responded in any number of ways, including the following potential inner dialogue:

"He thinks I'm ugly."

"That's interesting. I see me in the mirror every morning, and I don't think I'm ugly."

"That's too bad for him, because I'm a really fun person and a great friend. But probably not to people who think I'm ugly and are mean enough to let me know it."

"No one's ever told me I'm ugly before."

"In fact, people have told me I'm cute."

"Maybe he likes blondes."

"Maybe he prefers African-Americans, or Latinas, or Asians."

Or "Maybe he secretly thinks I'm hot and wants to run Mike off so *he* can ask me out."

Or even, "Maybe he really did just throw up in his mouth."

The point is my response to this simple event could have been any number of things that served me better than the one I had at the time. I could have talked myself through to the humor in the situation, but I *chose* to take the insult on the chin. I carried the "I'm ugly" thought around with me until some other external event "made" me start thinking otherwise (an invitation to a dance, a comment from a friend, etc.). I gave away my power to believe that I was attractive to a total stranger!

How often do we do this in life? How often do we allow external events to dictate our internal state of mind? How often do we feel like we're in *reaction* mode? How often do we feel that we can't do or feel what we want to because of the actions, or non-actions, of other people?

I'm going to share with you some ways to determine where you're giving your power away, where you're playing the victim instead of the owner of your life, and where you're not taking 100 percent responsibility for your life.

There are some easy clues to determine where you're not taking 100 percent responsibility for your own inner state, and they include the following: blaming, complaining, excuse making; your vocabulary; strong negative emotions; and results that you don't like.

Blaming, Complaining, and Excuse Making

Anytime we place blame on something or someone other than ourselves, we are failing to take responsibility for our own lives. Think about the list I provided earlier in this chapter:

Giving your power away: "My boss really frustrates me." This means that I'm giving my power of feeling accomplishment away to my boss.

Embracing your power: "I'm allowing my boss's actions to affect my emotions. I'll come up with a plan to express my ideas to her. If that doesn't help, then I'll try something else."

Giving your power away: "My sister really makes me angry," means I'm giving my sister the power over whether I feel at peace, or not.

Embracing your power: "I allow myself to feel used and angry when my sister borrows money and doesn't pay it back. I'll ask her to honor her commitments. If she won't, I'll stop loaning her money."

Giving your power away: "This always happens to me," means that I'm at the mercy of any and every external event that could possibly occur.

Embracing your power: "What am I doing to create this situation repeatedly in my life?"

Giving your power away: "I've tried to improve our marriage, but my spouse just won't change," means that I've signed away my power of feeling peace or happiness in my relationship completely to my spouse.

Embracing your power: "My spouse isn't ready for change, but I am. What can I do to bring more peace and contentment into the relationship, or into my own heart?"

Giving your power away: "Our house is always such a mess because my kids won't help out," means that my children are responsible for the state of my home.

Embracing your power: "I prefer a more orderly home, and I know that my children will benefit from being contributing members of the household. How can I engage them in being a part of the family team?"

Giving your power away: "I grew up eating this way, so I've always been overweight," means that I'm still blaming my parents for my current, poor eating habits.

Embracing your power: "While I certainly formed some poor eating habits in my youth, I'm free to choose habits that will serve my health better now."

Giving your power away: "I don't have time to do what I want because I have to help out at church every week," means that I'm blaming others for my inability to say no.

Embracing your power: "Agreeing to things because I think others expect it leads only to resentment. I can say no when saying yes interferes with my ability to follow my true calling."

Giving your power away: "I would be wealthy right now if the stock market hadn't crashed," means that others are responsible for making good financial decisions for me.

Embracing your power: "I alone am responsible for my financial health. What can I learn from the experience of losing my retirement account, and how can I avoid it ever happening again?"

Giving your power away: "This mess I'm in is all my ex's fault," means that my ex had and still has control over my own happiness.

Embracing your power: "I'll acknowledge my part in where I am right now, and I won't continue to allow my happiness to depend on anyone else's good or bad decisions."

Giving your power away: "My life was forever ruined when he raped me."

Embracing your power: "The reality is that he did something horrible to me in that moment, that he forced me to choose between being raped and being beaten or killed; but only I decide what, if anything at all, that says about the rest of my life. He has no power over me."

Can you see where placing blame on others for anything in our lives disempowers us? Our power is in taking ownership and responsibility for every part of our lives, from our happiness to our finances to our health.

Complaining initially may not sound like playing the victim. I mean, who among us hasn't complained from time to time, right? And how natural is it to be able to get things off our chest by complaining about them to a sympathetic listener?

However, the truth is that when we complain about something, it simply means that there is something out there that we are unwilling to take the risk of creating. Think about it for a moment. When I complain about the disorganized state of my desk, what am I comparing it to? I have an idea in my head of how I want my desk to look, but I haven't yet created that reality. Who am I assuming should fix it? The desk fairy?

The thing is, we normally complain about situations that are completely and totally within our power to change, but we often complain to the wrong person. We complain about our coworkers to our husband. We complain about our husband to our mother. We complain about our mother to our friends. And we complain about our friends to our other friends. Do we really want to fix anything?

If we did, we would talk to the appropriate person in order to bring about change. We would talk to our boss about our work. We would talk to our husband about our relationship. We would talk to our mother about our relationship with her, and we would never complain about a friend who wasn't in the room.

That is taking responsibility, becoming an owner of our lives, and embracing our power. Not only does this bring us much better results, but it also brings authenticity and integrity to all of our interactions and relationships.

Making excuses is another path to certain failure. It's been said that success slips through our fingers, one excuse at a time. When we commit to doing something, but we make excuses instead (whether to ourselves or to someone else), we take a step away from our dreams. You remember the discussion about self-esteem from the previous chapter? When we repeatedly fail to follow through on our commitments to ourselves, our self-esteem suffers. We lose self-trust. Success can only be achieved through forward action, and we only find excuses necessary when we've made no progress or have slipped backward. Take note of when you're making excuses. You've likely either just failed to follow through on a commitment that you shouldn't have agreed to in the first place, or you've just failed to take an action that would have brought you closer to your dreams.

A good example of this is the way many of us, myself included, often make excuses for our poor health and fitness habits. Do any of these sound familiar?

"It takes too much time to eat healthy."

"I need a nap more than exercise."

"It's too hot/cold/drizzly/windy to work out."

"I don't want to have to shower again today."

"I can't cook healthy meals because my family won't eat them."

Or how about the mother of all excuses—"I shouldn't have to eat healthy or work out while I'm on my period"? Yep, I've caught myself using this one. Incidentally, this one is a vortex that can suck the passion right out of you if you're not careful. It can be tempting to use this one to justify all manner of bad behavior, but it's a trap. Think of it as a soft, cozy blanket that gives you a full-body, stinging rash after you use it. It might make you feel better in the moment, but you'll certainly feel worse later.

By the way, I read a study recently that I thought you might find interesting:

A study has revealed that the kind of face a woman finds attractive on a man can differ, depending on where she is in her menstrual cycle. For example: If she is ovulating, she is attracted to men with rugged and masculine features. However, if she is menstruating or menopausal, she tends to be more attracted to a man with duct tape over his mouth and a spear lodged in his chest while he is on fire. No further studies are expected on the subject.

Fascinating stuff, huh?

Your Vocabulary

Another way that you can uncover areas where you give your power away is to become aware of your vocabulary. Anytime you use the words "can't," "couldn't," "should," "shouldn't," or "have to," watch out! You are headed toward victimhood and away from owning your own story, your own life.

Think of a task that you've been putting off or procrastinating. It can be anything—from doing last night's dishes to filing last year's tax return to making that phone call to an estranged family member. Say it out loud as an "I should" statement.

For example, "I should do last night's dishes"; "I should file last year's tax return"; or "I should call so-and-so."

Notice how saying that out loud makes you feel. Close your eyes while saying it, if that helps you get in touch with the feeling more easily.

Doesn't really inspire action, does it?

Now state it out loud as a choice, rather than an obligation.

For example, "I choose to do the dishes when I get home"; "I choose to file last year's tax return so I can cross it off my list"; or "I choose to call so-and-so to let her know I'm over it."

Notice how you feel now after stating it as a choice. Choosing to do something has a much more empowering feeling associated with it than doing something because we feel it's expected. In some cases, stating it as a choice can reveal that choosing *not* to do it makes more sense to you. Maybe you only have this particular task on your list because someone else expects you to do it. You may decide after this little exercise that you can cross something off your list without ever actually doing it, because, left up to you (which it always is), you'd never willingly *choose* to do it. Incidentally, I DO NOT recommend choosing to skip filing last year's tax return, since that would result in all kinds of new choices for you (like choosing between massive fines or extended jail time).

In all seriousness, though, realize that you are in fact choosing every action you take or don't take throughout your day and your life. Placing a "should" or a "can't" in front of your daily actions or inactions only serves to give you feelings of powerlessness and dread.

Strong Negative Emotions

Anytime you have strong negative emotions about something, step back and be aware. You're giving your power away. No one wants to feel fear, anger, disappointment, envy, inadequacy, or any other negative emotion. And yet, when we feel this way, we have *chosen* to do so. I know this is a tough one to swallow, but here's an example.

A few years ago, I noticed that I was feeling increasingly resentful toward my husband, because it seemed to me as if he was living his dream of building a business, while I was feeling more and more like I was merely playing a supporting role to his life. As my resentment grew and arguments ensued over silly things like the division of labor in our household, I gradually realized that if I was dissatisfied with my role in my own life, the only one who could change it was *me*. The resentment that was growing inside of me was really frustration with myself for not going after what I wanted. He was going after his dream, and I needed to do the same.

Let me assure you that coming to this painful realization was not easy, nor was it pleasant. It was excruciating to admit there was a part of me choosing to blame someone else, my husband, for my own failure to pursue my dreams. After all, I had always prided myself on my independence. I was master of my fate, right?

I found the following sentence in Nathaniel Branden's book *The Six Pillars of Self-Esteem*, and it spoke so profoundly to what I experienced in this incident that it jumped right off the page at me:

> The sad irony is that when people cease to honor their deepest needs and wants, they sometimes become selfish not in the noble but in the petty sense, grasping at trivia after they have surrendered their deeper yearnings, rarely even knowing what they have betrayed or given up.

Wow! Reading that still has the power to bring tears to my eyes because of its simple truth. I had become petty, not because of anything that my husband was or wasn't doing, but because of what *I* was and wasn't doing. I wasn't honoring my own deepest needs and wants. And it freaks me out a little bit to think that I might have continued to spiral in that direction, had I not discovered what I'm sharing with you here.

Fortunately, I did. Having grown through and overcome that mental and emotional challenge is what allows me to do what I'm now doing, which includes helping you do the same. On a personal level, my marriage is stronger for it. We have a much greater respect for each other, and I'm now following my passions.

Maybe you also have been struggling with resentment and frustration, never realizing that *you* are the key. That the answer is just there, inside of you. Try giving yourself a gut check when your anger, frustration, or jealousy gets intense. That strong emotion is trying to tell you something about yourself, if you'll only listen.

Results You Don't Like

When you experience results in your life with which you are completely dissatisfied—a crappy relationship, a substandard project completion at work, an unhealthy state of fitness, or a dismal financial situation—you have most likely failed to take 100 percent responsibility for your overall results in some way. For whatever reason, and maybe even in only a small way, you have not taken ownership of the situation. You have not created a result that left you feeling satisfied and fulfilled.

At the beginning of this chapter, I shared how I chose to embrace my power by walking away from an unhealthy relationship, even though it meant being a single parent at eighteen years old. In that moment, I took responsibility for my life and my son's life.

But later I understood that I had to take responsibility for getting myself into the situation in the first place. Not in the sense that I needed to beat myself up over it, but that I needed to recognize my own mistakes so that I didn't repeat them.

In order to grow from it, I had to own that I had allowed myself to get into that mess—pregnant at eighteen by a guy who drank too much and liked to punch people. Clarity actually had tried a more gentle approach, but I hadn't listened, hadn't opened my eyes, hadn't trusted my gut feelings. So clarity had to take more drastic measures to get my attention. *Touché.*

Now that you know that it's all within your power, you can easily avoid receiving a long-overdue slap from clarity. Review the work you did in Chapter 3 where you assessed what's currently not working in your life. Ask yourself if you're taking 100 percent responsibility for it. Not so you can feel bad about it, but so you can make course corrections and start moving in the direction of what you DO want. Specifically, take out your Sexy Little Twist journal and ask yourself the following question. Then write down the first five or six answers that come to you:

"If I were to take just 5 percent more responsibility for _____ (insert area of dissatisfaction here, i.e., my financial situation, my relationship with so-and-so, my career path, etc.), then I would . . ."

Don't overthink it; just jot down whatever bubbles up. Without making any physical changes, this will help tremendously in developing a new mindset that positive change is completely within your control. Better yet—put a plan in place to take action on those items that came to you.

Sexy Little Twists of Ownership and Responsibility

- Our power is in how we think, feel, and act.
- Be the owner of your life, not a victim.
- Your response is the only thing you can change in order to get a different outcome (E + R = O).
- Dump blaming, complaining, and excuse making down the drain.
- Add a splash of "I choose" to your vocabulary.
- Work on taking just 5 percent more responsibility and you'll be amazed at the difference.
- If you're unsure about a tough decision, don't sweat it. Clarity has a wicked backhand.

Girl Talk (or Journaling Exercises):

Think of a time when you felt insulted, angry, or hurt over something that another person did or said. Share the incident with the group and discuss alternative internal responses (Rs) that you might have had that would have changed the outcome for you. Be sure to create at least one humorous response to the incident.

Think of a time when you took responsibility for the outcome of a project, event, incident, or situation. Share it with the group and discuss how you felt about the result. How did it affect your belief that you could make a difference in other areas?

Think of an area of your life that you feel could use some improvement—career, finances, relationships, fitness, or whatever. Plug that area into the blank below and then provide five endings to the sentence:

"If I were to take just 5 percent more responsibility for my <u>blank</u>, I would . . ."

Share your five sentences with the group.

Take turns finishing the sentence "I should . . ." Go around the group three times, remembering what your sentences were. Then take turns saying the same sentences, except begin with the words "I choose to . . ." instead of "I should . . ." Discuss with the group the difference you felt in saying, "I choose to" versus "I should."

Take turns finishing the sentence "I can't . . ." As before, go around the group three times, remembering what your sentences were. Now take turns saying the same sentences, except begin with the words "I choose not to . . ." instead of "I can't." Discuss with the group the difference you felt in saying, "I choose not to" versus "I can't."

Discuss how you will use the concepts in this chapter to elevate and improve your results and your life. Commit to one small change that you will make in your daily or weekly habits and be prepared to discuss your experience at the next meeting.

Chapter 7

It's Not Bragging if It's True!

"Living is like tearing through a museum. Not until later do you really start absorbing what you saw, thinking about it, looking it up in a book, and remembering—because you can't take it in all at once."

—Audrey Hepburn

W e've done a lot of exploring what hasn't worked for us in the past. By now, you've acknowledged the reality of where you are and what you think needs to change in order for you to experience a comeback in your life. You've examined some past mistakes and are now holding the hope that things can turn around for you.

The next step in the process is to acknowledge the successes that you've had. And don't tell me you don't have any. You do, but you're probably not giving yourself credit for them. Or perhaps you've just never stopped running long enough to celebrate them. Well, that's what we're going to do now. For several reasons:

1. Living life with a Sexy Little Twist requires that we look at ourselves in a new way. Our old beliefs and self-image got us where we are now. Which is good, but maybe not fabulous (or you wouldn't have picked up this book).

2. We want to continue to think the thoughts, feel the feelings, and take the actions that have worked for us in the past. We don't want to throw out the baby with the bathwater, so to speak.

3. We spend far too much of our energy beating ourselves up over our failures, and it's time to even things up.

4. Acknowledging our successes has a direct impact on our level of self-esteem.

5. Moving into the next phase of a living life with a Sexy Little Twist requires that we be in a positive, grateful, open-minded state. In the next chapters, we'll be dreaming about the future and setting new, exciting goals. We want to be in an expansive state of mind for these exercises, and acknowledging our successes will help us do just that.

Our culture tends to focus more on what's going wrong than on what's going right. In parenting, we spend more time telling our kids how *not to* act than how *to* act. We tend to get more passionate (negatively) when our kids mess up than we do (positively) about them doing the right thing. In school, the wrong answers are marked, not the right ones. Parents are called when a student is doing poorly in a subject, not when they're doing well. "Getting called to the principal's office" is a tradition in our culture that fills kids with dread. At work, employees are generally expected to do a good job. Much like the principal's office, getting called to the boss's office conjures up images of reprimands, performance plans, and unemployment. Good behavior is expected; bad behavior is addressed.

And this is not to pick on parents, teachers, and employers. It's a phenomenon born of expediency rather than evil intent. It's just quicker to point out the flaws, because they are, in reality, rarer than strengths. In the example of a math test, it's generally quicker to mark the wrong answers than the right ones. The truth is, on any given day, we have *far* more successes than failures. It's just a part of our makeup that we *expect* success on a regular basis and only panic when our expectation isn't met, when we fail. So we are completely out of practice with acknowledging, appreciating, and celebrating our successes.

It also is true that we remember well anything with which we associate strong emotions. Think about the following scenario:

You've committed to being the secretary of the Parent/Teacher Association at your son's grade school. You prepare an agenda for the meetings each month. You show up to the monthly meetings, type up the minutes, and email them to everyone on the list. You repeat this pattern every month for the entire school year.

But in the month of April, you somehow didn't get the meeting onto your calendar and forgot about it. You didn't give it a thought until ten minutes after the meeting had started, when you received a phone call from the PTA president asking where you were. You're in the middle of having dinner with your family or you're in the grocery store or you're in your pajamas already, curled up with a book. Regardless, you're not going to make the meeting, and someone else is going to have to take the minutes for you.

Now, is your overall feeling about this scenario one of success or failure? If you're like most of us, you're feeling only the guilt or embarrassment or anxiety about not meeting your commitment or letting people down. You're worried about who will have to take the minutes and whether they'll be feeling resentment toward you that they're doing your job.

So, for eight months you've racked up numerous successes that you could acknowledge and celebrate. But because those only get lumped into a dull "doing what's expected," they don't count nearly as much as the one time that you *didn't* do what was expected. When it's time to volunteer for the next school year, will your mind automatically flash to the guilt or embarrassment over your failure to make that one meeting? It's quite possible. The strong negative feeling of that one embarrassing failure could very well overshadow the contribution you made the rest of the year. And mostly because of the varying level of intensity of the associated feelings.

Do you see my point? Now I'm not trying to say that we should get carried away and celebrate every time we manage to floss our teeth. But I am saying that we would do well to focus a lot more on what we're doing well in order to keep our failures in proper perspective.

The "Look at Me Go!" Exercise

So let's do an exercise to help convince you that you are already a successful person. We'll call it the "Look at Me Go!" exercise. I want you to pull out your journal and list a minimum of one hundred successes you've achieved in your life.

Yep, that's right. One. Hundred.

The first few will probably be easy. These will be the ones for which other people have acknowledged you—getting a promotion, winning an award, finishing a project. Then you may have to ponder a bit. You'll come up with some successes that you forgot about, perhaps some from when you were much younger, or maybe some that you didn't realize were successes until much later. After that, you may get stuck. You'll be at the place where you'll need to recognize successes you've had, but that no one else acknowledged or even knows about—overcoming an emotional challenge, making a tough decision, dropping a bad habit. Once you get to this place, you'll be home free and may not want to stop at one hundred. I can tell you from personal experience that reaching one hundred is an accomplishment in and of itself (in fact, my 103rd success was that I completed the list). Putting these successes on paper is a great boost to self-esteem and contributes greatly to a sense of accomplishment, which is a great state of mind to carry into the next chapters.

So, put the book down and spend about ten minutes writing down everything you can think of off the top of your head. It's okay if you want to spread this exercise out over two or three days, but be sure to complete it before you move on to the exercises in the next chapter.

Your Environment

Let's talk about the environment in which you work, play, and live. Research tells us that our environment has a great deal of influence over us. An extreme example is discussed in Malcolm Gladwell's book *The Tipping Point*, where the drop in crime rate in New York City's subway system (in the 1980s) actually can be attributed to the city's concerted effort to clean up the subway—painting over graffiti, etc. Changing the environment actually affected behavior.

Look around you. Does your environment lift you up or pull you down? Do you display your successes so that you can draw regularly from the positive feelings associated with them?

I worked for a large corporation for a number of years, and I had a stack of certificates that I'd received for various things—quarterly employee awards, kudos for finishing big projects, and certifications for courses I had completed. Where did I keep them all? In a file in my desk drawer of course! I had two theories about hanging them on the wall:

1. Hanging them on the wall was a form of showing off. I didn't want to be seen as conceited.
2. Whatever I had done to receive an award or certificate was in the past. I told myself that it was my way of keeping me hungry to achieve the next thing. As if appreciating what I had accomplished would cause me to rest on my laurels, so to speak. I thought that a constant reminder of the great things I had done in the past would make me lazy in the present!

All right, so I can admit to that embarrassing bit of self-psychology, because I know better now. And if you found yourself identifying with either of the reasons above for not displaying your successes, I'm here to convince you you're wrong.

To address my first theory, the truth is that displaying your successes isn't about showing off to other people at all. And anyone who would walk into your space and think you're showing off with all your success evidence wallpapered around you simply doesn't understand how the human mind works and could use the guidance that you'll now be able to offer them. It's not about other people, because it's about YOU and how the memorabilia makes YOU feel! And to be honest, the whole premise of worrying about what others will think is a mentality you'll need to rid yourself of in order to live life with a Sexy Little Twist. Others will think what they'll think. There's literally nothing that can, or should, be done about that. But also, what keeps you from conceit is gratitude, which we'll talk about shortly. Just know for now that you can be humble and still display your successes at the same time. I promise!

As for the second theory, I was so far off base it's laughable. In fact, by adapting an attitude of "that's in the past; file it and stay on your toes," I likely was sabotaging all of my future efforts. Abundance and success don't come from a place of lack and failure. I thought that if I got too proud of myself, I would cease to accomplish things of which to be proud. In fact, the opposite is true. Success begets more success. It is not when we are consumed with fear of failure that we succeed. Oh sure, I may have continued to receive awards, but all that proved was that I could make *others* notice my efforts. This is a far cry from experiencing my own sense of accomplishment, my own sense of fulfillment, and my own sense of peace and purpose. And though I left corporate America while I was still riding that high of recognition, I truly believe that it eventually would have taken a toll, that sooner or later I would have discovered the emptiness and exhaustion of constantly moving on to the next thing, the next success, the next proof of my value. Because at the basic level, I wasn't operating from a sense of how successful I already was. I was operating from a place of still having to prove my value to myself (and others). And this is not where continued success comes from.

To illustrate my point, think back now on one major thing that you have accomplished in your life. Doesn't matter what it is—having a baby, getting a promotion, finishing a big project, losing ten pounds, learning to drive, speaking a different language, or picking up a new hobby. You pick something that resonates with you, something that gives you a feeling of satisfaction, pride, or accomplishment. Got it?

Okay, now what state of mind were you in as you were making it happen? Were you feeling like a failure, a loser, someone who never accomplishes anything they set out to do? Doubt it! You were in a positive state of mind, believing that you could make it happen. Sure, you might've been scared or anxious that it might not turn out the way you hoped, and maybe it didn't exactly. But in general, you had hope and determination that you could make it happen, and you did!

This is the state that we put ourselves in when we surround ourselves with evidence of our successes. So go ahead, girl! Find a spot in your home or office or cube or bathroom and create a success collage. Don't give a moment's consideration to how other people will view what you hang on your wall. Yours is the only opinion that matters. Post those certificates, awards, or degrees. If you just thought, "But it's only an associate degree," then give yourself "the look" (you know, the one that says, "Oh no, you didn't"). Realize that the challenges you overcame to get it may well surpass the challenges someone else overcame to get a doctorate. Put it up there! Post pictures of that vacation you arranged, that thank-you note from a friend or a local community organization, that small write-up in the paper about your essay or artwork in school, those badges from Girl Scouts. Include pictures of your trophies from sports or that first car you bought and paid for yourself. And you have my permission to post copies of your kids' degrees and awards, since you likely had a heavy hand in helping them achieve them. I've got copies of my sons' Second Degree Black Belt Certificates from the American Taekwondo Association on my success wall. Though the sweat and determination was all theirs, it wouldn't have happened without my willingness to spend the money on classes, testing, and equipment, and the time and energy to get them to class week after week, year after year. Point is, if you feel good about your contribution to it, post it!

As a side note, this is a great project to help your kids complete. Let them create a success wall in their bedroom or in the hallway.

And every day when you walk by your success collage, soak up the energy from it. Absorb the feelings of accomplishment and pride that you get from all the things you've done. You'll be amazed—not only at how it makes you feel, but also at the impact it will have on your attitude toward making more things happen in your life. You've already done amazing things; celebrate them! This brings us to the next point of acknowledging our successes—rewarding ourselves.

Reward Yourself

When we reward ourselves for a job well done, we complete the cycle of success. Sometimes, the job just doesn't feel complete until this happens. Have you ever promised yourself a new pair of jeans if you lost five pounds, and then failed to deliver once the goal was achieved? Maybe you moved right on to another goal of losing another five pounds. You probably told yourself that you didn't want a pair of jeans that would be too big once you lost that second five pounds anyway. But just like this failure to honor commitments would eventually cause a small child to distrust, the same is true of your inner self. After a while, even you don't believe what you promise. Believe it or not, this failure to reward for a job well done creates just a tiny bit of mental clutter, a slight ding in your self-esteem, if you'll remember. In addition, it robs us of the sense of accomplishment that could very well boost us into our next endeavor.

Don't wait for someone else to do it. If someone else acknowledges you for your efforts, consider it a bonus. Again, only you know the effort you put into making something happen.

It doesn't have to be anything major, or costly, or fattening (though it could be, if that makes your heart sing). Let the level of effort or accomplishment be your guide. If you've done a small favor for someone, do a small favor for yourself. If you're buying flowers for a relative in the hospital, then buy some for you, too. If you finally cleaned out and organized your garage, schedule a massage for yourself. And if you've spent six months working overtime to launch a new website for your company, then by all means, take a few days off and do something fun. But acknowledge that you made it happen and reward yourself accordingly. It feels good in the moment, it boosts your self-esteem, and it puts you in a great mindset for your next attempt at *anything*. And it's a great reminder that you're not at the mercy of anyone else's benevolence. If you take time to acknowledge yourself, then you can totally skip the feelings of disappointment and frustration that no one else noticed your efforts.

Gratitude

"If the only prayer you ever say in your whole life is
'thank you,' that would suffice."
—Meister Eckhart

I mentioned earlier in this chapter that one way to avoid conceit is through gratitude. So let's talk about this for a moment.

It's difficult to convey within a single chapter all of the benefits of living in a state of gratitude. Numerous books have been written on this topic alone. While this is not a book about gratitude, I can't stress enough the impact that it will have on your ability to live life with a Sexy Little Twist.

Dr. Robert Emmons, known as a leading expert on the subject, has been studying gratitude and its effects for many years and has written books on the topic. One of the key elements of gratitude is the acknowledgement that the good things that happen in your life don't necessarily come from within. Nothing is created in a vacuum. No man (or woman) is an island. When you recognize that you've been given gifts, support, blessings, etc. (whether you believe they've come from God or from others), and you're grateful for the gifts, then you will never be consumed by the conceit I had feared back in my corporate days. The two emotions of gratitude and conceit are incompatible and cannot reside simultaneously in the same heart.

Dr. Emmons and his colleagues have found that gratitude offers us many other benefits, including:

- Increased levels of well-being and happiness.
- Increased levels of energy, optimism, and empathy.
- A reminder of all the positive things in our life.
- The ability to turn bad things into good ones, as in being grateful for growth and learning opportunity from disappointments or failures.
- A reminder of what's important to us—as in not sweating the small daily mishaps when we're grateful that our family is healthy.
- A reminder to thank others, which makes them happy, which in turn makes us happy.
- Strengthened relationships from openly acknowledging how others have supported us.

Gratitude promotes forgiveness, makes us more resilient in rebounding from setbacks, allows us to celebrate the present moment, and causes us to be more helpful and compassionate toward others.

Surprisingly, there are also physical benefits to gratitude. It can help reduce anxiety and depression. It strengthens our immune system, lowers our blood pressure, reduces symptoms of illness, and helps us sleep better.

Wow, right?

I can hear you now, "So, Danne, how can I get me some more of this gratitude stuff? Sounds like a miracle drug!"

Well, you're in luck because Dr. Emmons' research also has revealed that gratitude *can* be deliberately improved, which you already know if you've ever tried it. No research grant required.

Here are a few actions you can take to improve your gratitude skills:

- Keep a gratitude journal. I know this one seems cliché by now; but seriously, if you've never tried it, do it now. If you've tried it before, but fell out of the habit, pick it up again. Once a day, write down five things you're grateful for. I do this every day, and it never fails to boost my mood and color my interactions with others directly after.

- Start a morning gratitude ritual. Before getting out of bed each morning, call to mind something, anything for which you're truly grateful. Ronda Byrne, creator of the film *The Secret*, states that she doesn't get out of bed each morning *until* she's in a mental state of gratitude.

- Acknowledge and appreciate someone every day. Let someone know, whether in person, on the phone, over email, or Facebook, that you really appreciate them. You may feel awkward at first because it's something you feel you should've said long ago or it's just not how you're accustomed to speaking. Do it anyway! Don't be shy, and *do* be specific about what you appreciate; you're going to be amazed at how good they, and you, feel after you've said it. I learned this little action from Jack Canfield, creator of the *Chicken Soup for the Soul* series and co-author of *The Success Principles*.

He has participants do this for homework each night during his seminars. The energy created by a hotel filled with appreciative and appreciated people is difficult to describe on paper. Check it out for yourself.

- Give thanks for the negative. Remember in Chapter 3 when we learned to look at our mistakes and ask ourselves, "What is the learning opportunity in this?" That is what I mean by giving thanks for the negative. Gratitude becomes our modus operandi when we are thankful for the growth opportunities we get from our setbacks.

- Learn a gratitude prayer. Learn it, feel it, memorize it, and use it often to evoke gratitude when you feel anything but.

- Use visual or tactile reminders. In Joe Vitale's book *The Key: The Missing Secret for Attracting Anything You Want,* he shares how he used a simple rock in his pocket to remind himself to be grateful. Like Joe, you can keep something in your environment that will remind you to get back into the state of gratitude. It might be a sticky note on your bathroom mirror, a trinket hanging from the rearview mirror of your car, or even a bracelet you wear regularly. Here's a challenge—if it's not already, turn your wedding ring into a reminder to be grateful for the amazing person you married. See if that doesn't inspire a Sexy Little Twist in your relationship.

Your exercise for this chapter is to pick at least one of the actions listed above and do it every day for a week. At the end of the week, pull out your Sexy Little Twist journal and spend ten minutes writing about what you learned from it. Did you see or feel any improvements in your life? How about physically—did you notice any difference in your energy level or your ability to sleep? Did you have any moments with others when your gratitude had an impact on your interaction? Did your gratitude rub off on anyone? If you verbally appreciated someone, how did they react? Can you see benefits to making this a permanent habit, and what would those be?

Sexy Little Twists of Success and Thankfulness

- Acknowledging our successes has a direct impact on our self-esteem.
- Contemplating our successes and surrounding ourselves with evidence of them inspires us into actions that help us to experience more of them.
- Rewarding ourselves for a job well done completes the cycle of success so that we can move confidently on to our next challenge.
- Our Martini of Life will taste sour without the indispensable ingredient of gratitude.

Girl Talk (or Journaling Exercises):

Share three successes from your list with the group. Discuss how you felt about the success when it occurred, as well as how it makes you feel to think back on it now.

If you already have a "brag board," share with the group where it is and what you have posted on it. If you don't already have one, discuss what you would post on it if you created one. Where would you place it and why?

Review your list of successes and find one that you feel you haven't properly rewarded yourself for accomplishing. Discuss with the group how you will correct that oversight. How will you reward yourself for it now?

Share the results from your gratitude experiment with the group. What did you learn? How did it affect your interactions with others? Did you notice any physical effects, and if so, what were they? If you verbally appreciated someone, share with the group how they reacted.

Discuss how you will use the concepts in this chapter to elevate and improve your results and your life. Commit to one small change that you will make in your daily or weekly habits and be prepared to discuss your experience at the next meeting.

Chapter 8

Sexy on Purpose

"Don't ask yourself what the world needs. Ask yourself
what makes you come alive and then go do that. Because
what the world needs is people who have come alive."
—Howard Thurman

"The world needs that special gift that only you have."
—Marie Forleo

From the beginning of time, men and women have asked the question, "Why am I here?" Contrary to popular belief, we *can* discern the answer. As I stated in the Introduction, I've made my living in numerous different roles over the years. Sometimes when I took on a new role (such as becoming a truck driver), I acknowledged that it was merely a temporary situation, something that was a means to an end. Other times, such as when I became a financial planner, I had hopes that it would be a career, a calling that would help me to feel fulfilled for a long time, if not the rest of my life.

But something about each situation that I landed in revealed that it just wasn't the perfect fit for me. Something about it wasn't quite what I had hoped for or expected. None of them felt like what I was supposed to be when I grew up.

After so many of those failed attempts to discover what I was meant to be, I started to worry that I would never figure it out. I began having thoughts like, "What if I grow old and die having never figured out what my purpose was?" And then, "What if I DO discover my life's purpose and realize that I've wasted half of my life going in the wrong direction?" Both thoughts were equally terrifying. Terrifying in a sad and depressing sort of way. Ultimately, I suppose the thought of never discovering my purpose was more frightening than the thought that I had wasted a couple of decades first.

As I begin the topic of life purpose, I want to first give a shout out to Rick Warren, author of *A Purpose Driven Life*, and others of equal genius in the realm of spirituality. Having reached a level of spirituality that I only aspire to at this point in my life, Rick would likely consider what I'm calling life purpose a "life's work." So I fully acknowledge the possibility that there is a higher plane of purpose to my life beyond what I can grasp with my current, puny level of enlightenment. Many gurus would say here that the purpose of our lives is merely to "be." But that is more esoteric and philosophical than what I want to convey to you here. What I mean by purpose in this context is what I understand as the deepest calling of my soul, what I feel I was brought into this world to do. I'm using the term *purpose* here to imply *action*, rather than simply *existence*.

Having said that, understand that I'm not advocating that your life purpose needs to be a specific activity, such as to paint portraits or drive race cars, though painting portraits or driving race cars could easily be an expression of your life purpose.

When I use the term purpose, I'm talking about something on a philosophical level—somewhere between simply "being" and "driving race cars."

Life purpose has to do with how we use our gifts to serve others, to make a contribution to the world. If your life purpose doesn't include an acknowledgement of how others (or even one other) benefit from your gifts, it's not quite finished yet. Thus, painting portraits and driving race cars are not quite full as life purposes.

Ultimately, we aren't here to serve ourselves. We're here to serve others by honoring ourselves. We were given gifts because the world needs what we have. As the quote at the beginning of this chapter indicates, the best way to serve is to figure out what we love to do and then develop ways to use those talents in the service of others.

If you already know your life purpose, congratulations! You've already experienced what I'm about to say. If you don't know your life purpose yet, get ready to be amazed!

Nothing will bring more passion, determination, and joy to your everyday activities, present and future, than knowing and feeling your life purpose at a gut level. And quite the opposite of what I used to believe, having perfect clarity on my life purpose actually made sense of all of my previous rambling, seemingly unconnected roles and jobs. Knowing what I know now, it's perfectly clear to me how I have benefited from everything that I've done in the past. Every role I've played in my history has contributed in some way, large or small, to my ability to now carry out my purpose, which I share at the end of this book.

As with many of the other topics discussed in this book, there are numerous books written on discovering your life purpose. I'm going to cover several of my favorite methods here to get you started on the path to discovering your own life purpose.

This first exercise is from Jack Canfield's book, *The Success Principles* (originally created by Arnold M. Patent, spiritual coach and author of *You Can Have It All*). Jack says that we're born with an inner guidance system. This system tells us when we are on or off purpose by the amount of joy we are experiencing. What brings you joy is in alignment with your purpose.

So, take out your Sexy Little Twist journal and set a timer for ten minutes. Spend the entire time making a list of the times you have felt most joyful and alive. Don't think too hard; just make the list. When the ten minutes are up, review your list and think about what the common elements of those activities are. Then work through the following steps:

1. List two of your unique personal qualities, such as *enthusiasm* and *creativity.*

2. List one or two ways you enjoy expressing those qualities when interacting with others, such as *to encourage* or *to inspire.*

3. Imagine your perfect world right now. What does this world look like? How is everyone interacting with everyone else? What does it feel like? Write your answer as a statement, in the present tense, describing the ultimate condition, the perfect world as you see it and feel it. Remember, a perfect world is a fun place to be.

    Example: Everyone is confident and relaxed. Everyone is achieving their goals and living their dreams. Everyone appreciates, enjoys, and benefits from the talents and gifts of others.

4. Combine the three prior subdivisions of this list into a single statement.

    Example: My purpose is to use my authenticity and creativity to inspire and encourage others to live their dreams by sharing their gifts with the world.

So this single statement encapsulates your own unique life purpose. If you're like me, you're now looking at that statement with a bit of skepticism. When I first completed this exercise, I thought, "Can it really be that easy? What if it's wrong? What if I really buy into it and then find out later that it wasn't my life purpose after all?"

So, me being me, I set out to find more evidence that what I came up with was, in fact, my true life purpose. I discovered and tried many other methods, a few of which I'll share below. But what I found was that, with a few minor tweaks, my original purpose was pretty close to perfect.

But here's the important thing (are you paying attention?)—ultimately, no matter what you come up with, it becomes a *choice* to make that your life purpose. The bottom line is that even a slightly imperfect life purpose is a great deal sexier than having no purpose at all. So, move determinedly in the direction of the one you have. Embrace it and live it. It will serve you perfectly until you discover that it needs an adjustment. Then you'll make the modification, embrace it, and live it. No harm, no foul.

Having said that, here are a few other methods for determining your life purpose, or for verifying one, as I did.

Meditation

Find a quiet place to sit comfortably where you won't be interrupted. Close your eyes and do your best to empty your mind of all thoughts of past, present, or future. Try to just "be." When you're feeling peaceful and relaxed, ask yourself (or God, if that resonates better for you), *What is the purpose of my life?* Or *What is my unique role in the universe?* Let the answer just come to you. Don't worry about it sounding poetic or eloquent. And don't worry if nothing comes, or if something unexpected comes to you. You may need to repeat this meditation quite a few times, especially if you are new to the practice. In fact, you may want to repeat it several times, even if you get an answer during your first attempt. When you've nailed it, you'll begin getting the same answer again and again. If you feel disappointed or let down in any way by the answer, you haven't discovered your purpose yet. You'll know you have it when you feel inspired and enthusiastic. A true life purpose will make you feel energized and joyful.

Guided Meditations

There are recorded meditations designed specifically to talk you through discovering your life purpose. I've used Jack Canfield's and Dr. Deb Sandella's "Being Clear Why You're Here" meditation on their *Awakening Power* CD. This one guides you up the side of a mountain to a beautiful temple where an item in a golden box helps reveal to you your life purpose. As you contemplate the item in the box, you discern what its significance is in the fulfillment of your life, which in turn helps you find clarity on your purpose.

The Passion Test

Another popular method is found in the book *The Passion Test: The Effortless Path to Discovering Your Destiny*, by Janet Bray Attwood and Chris Attwood. This method is slightly different, in that you end up with a short but powerful list of things you are truly, deeply passionate about, rather than a single statement like the exercise you completed above. At its core, The Passion Test is a simple method of making a list of ten or more things that you truly love to do, things that really bring you joy when you're doing them; and then, through a process of elimination, paring the list down to your top five. The official Passion Test gets into a bit more detail, but that's the essence of it. You end up with a short list of things that you care deeply about, and you recognize that they represent your purpose in life.

Regardless of how you arrive at your life purpose statement(s), once you've determined your purpose, write it down. Post it in a place you'll see it frequently, like your refrigerator, bathroom mirror, or the dashboard of your car. Read it every morning and make a commitment to living out your purpose in your daily activities. Without a deep-rooted belief in your life purpose, you may find yourself wandering through your day or your life, as I once did, without a sense of direction. With it, you will understand how you can live your purpose through big actions, such as starting a foundation, as well as through mundane activities, such as doing your laundry and mowing the lawn. And I'm not exaggerating.

Let's use the example from the exercise above, since it's mine (until I tweak it again). My life purpose is *to use my authenticity and creativity to inspire and encourage people to live their dreams by sharing their gifts with the world.*

So, how do I live that while I'm doing the laundry? I find creative ways to get more efficient and effective at it, so that I can spend more time living my purpose and my family can spend more time living theirs. Since it's my sanctuary and my primary environment, it's important to me (and to fully living my purpose) that my home is peaceful, organized, and that my family and I wear clean clothes. Rather than a dreaded chore, I can look at laundry as a means to an end. In gratitude, I often also recall that there was a time in my life when I couldn't afford a washer and dryer; so I spent an entire evening each week at a laundromat, a young toddler in tow. By comparison, what I do now is downright pleasant.

Take a fresh look at your dreaded chores and see if you can't find the higher purpose that they serve in your life. What would be the alternative? If you stopped doing them, what would that look like eventually?

In her book *Happy for No Reason*, Marci Shimoff shares a parable about a woman walking down the street and passing three men laying bricks with mortar.

She asks the first what he is doing, to which he replies, "I'm laying these bricks, obviously." She asks the second what he is doing, and he replies, "I'm earning money to feed my family." When she asks the third man the same question, he replies, "I'm building this beautiful cathedral."

All three were doing the exact same activity, but each, in his own mind, had given the activity a different meaning, a different purpose. *That*, my friend, is how you live your life purpose by doing the dishes. You find the higher purpose in the activity.

Now that we've established your life purpose (and again, no worries, just go with it even if you're still not 100 percent convinced it's perfect), in the next chapters we will explore and develop an amazing vision for your future. We will look at what you want to do, be, and have, so that we can put together plans for achieving your dreams.

Sexy Little Twists of Purpose

- Life purpose is about honoring our own gifts in order to serve ourselves and others.
- Finding clarity in your life purpose makes sense of your past.
- An imperfect life purpose statement is sexier than no life purpose at all.
- Even your dreaded chores are a means to you living your life purpose.

Girl Talk (or Journaling Exercises):

Share your life purpose statement with the group. Explain which exercise(s) or method(s) you used to develop it. If you used more than one, did your life purpose evolve; and if so, in what ways? How does it make you feel about your past to know what this is? How does it make you feel about your future?

Make a list of three to five endings for the following sentence: "If I were to more fully live my life purpose, I would . . ." Share your answers with the group. Brainstorm with the group other activities that each of you might do in order to live your life purpose more fully.

Write down one chore that you do on a regular basis but absolutely dread. Next, write three ways that having this chore completed contributes to your ability to live your life purpose. Share what you wrote with the group and get feedback on other possible benefits. Brainstorm ideas on how you might avoid doing this task yourself, through delegation, paying someone else to do it, etc.

Discuss how you will use the concepts in this chapter to elevate and improve your results and your life. Commit to one small change that you will make in your daily or weekly habits and be prepared to discuss your experience at the next meeting.

Chapter 9

What's This Party Gonna Look Like?

"The future belongs to those who believe in the beauty of their dreams."
—Eleanor Roosevelt

N ow comes the fun part! This is where we get to daydream about what we really want out of life! And by we, I mean YOU! And that doesn't mean what your husband wants, what your parents want, what your kids want, or what your friends want. This is about *your* vision and *your* desires. And I want you to promise me, and yourself, that you will abolish any guilt or anxiety about thinking only of yourself throughout this entire chapter! I know this will be hard for you, because we generally are not conditioned to think this way. If it's too much of a stretch for you, just remember that the best way you can serve others is to honor yourself! You are your gift to the world, to your family, your friends, and your community. Denying the world the beauty of YOU is the most selfish thing you can do.

What we're going to do in this chapter is develop a vision for how you want your life to be. You may be familiar with this technique from a business perspective. Companies describe what success looks like from the perspective of a few years into the future. We're going to take this concept and apply it to various aspects of our lives—from relationships to finances, from fitness to spirituality.

Ground Rules

First, I want to clarify some ground rules:

1. This is *your* vision, not anyone else's. I know I said this already, but it bears repeating. It makes no sense to develop a vision that would only excite your mother. She can develop her own vision; this one's yours.
2. Play full out. If you catch yourself making your vision smaller because your initial thought doesn't seem plausible, stop! It doesn't take any more energy to dream big than to dream small. Stick with your original vision; that's where your joy is.
3. Vision is about *what*, not *how*. Don't trouble yourself for now with concerns about how you could possibly accomplish your vision. The vision comes first; we'll get to the *how* later.
4. Don't let anyone talk you out of it. There will always be people who will try to talk you out of what you want. They'll tell you it's too ambitious, too big, and too weird. Refer to Rule #1. What may seem ambitious or crazy to them might be perfectly in line with your own purpose and vision. History is loaded with successful people who were ridiculed on the way up.

Plan to spend a minimum of fifteen minutes completing this exercise. I recommend finding a spot where you can feel a little inspiration, perhaps a park, a library, or the beach. Unless you are an expert meditator, who can completely tune out your environment, don't attempt this at your kitchen table surrounded by stacks of paperwork, piles of dirty laundry, and a sink full of dirty dishes. Trust me, the mental clutter will negatively influence your vision.

Pull out your Sexy Little Twist journal and sit quietly for a few moments. When you're in a peaceful, relaxed, or joyful state, ask your subconscious mind to show you images of what your life would look like if you could have it exactly the way you want it. As the images come to you, begin writing what you see (excerpted from Jack Canfield's *The Success Principles*):

1. First, focus on the financial area of your life. What is your annual income? What does your cash flow look like? How much money do you have in savings and investments? What is your total net worth?

    What does your home look like? Where is it located? Does it have a view? What kind of yard and landscaping does it have? Is there a pool or a stable for horses? What color are the walls? What type of flooring is in each room? What does the furniture look like? Are there paintings hanging in the rooms? What do they look like? Walk through your perfect house, filling in all of the details.

    Remember not to worry for now about how you'll make this vision happen.

2. Next, visualize your ideal job or career. Where are you working? Are you traveling? If so, where? What are you doing? With whom are you working? What kind of clients or customers do you have? What are you helping them do? What is your compensation like? Is it your own business?

3. Then, focus on your free time, your recreation time. What are you doing with your family and friends in the free time you've created for yourself? What hobbies are you pursuing? What kinds of vacations do you take? What do you do for fun?

4. Next, what is your ideal vision of your body and your physical health? Are you free of all disease? What age do you live to? Are you open, relaxed, in an ecstatic state of bliss all day long? Are you full of energy and vitality? Are you flexible as well as strong? What do you weigh? What size clothes do you wear? Do you exercise, eat good food, and drink lots of water?

5. Then move on to your ideal vision of your relationships with your family and friends. What is your relationship with your family like? How much time do you spend together, and what do you do? How do you interact with each other? Who are your friends? What is the quality of your relationships with your friends? What do those friendships feel like? Are they loving, supportive, empowering? What kinds of things do you do together?

6. What about the personal arena of your life? Do you see yourself going back to school, getting training, attending workshops, seeking therapy for a past hurt, or growing spiritually? Do you meditate or go on spiritual retreats with your church? Do you want to learn to play an instrument or write your autobiography? Do you want to run a marathon or take an art class? Do you want to travel to other countries?

7. Finally, focus on the community you live in, the community you've chosen. What does it look like when it is operating perfectly? What kinds of community activities take place there? What about your charitable work? What do you do to help others and make a difference? How often do you participate in these activities? Who are you helping?

Review what you've written on a regular basis—daily, if possible, weekly at a minimum. In the next chapter, we'll talk about how to transform this vision into solid objectives to work toward. For now, by reading your vision on a regular basis, your subconscious mind will go to work solving the issue of how to get there. Remember in Chapter 2 when we talked about your Reticular Activating System (RAS)? Reviewing this vision often will start opening your mind to the possibilities out there for turning your dreams into reality.

Sharing Your Vision

If you really want to solidify your vision, share it with a trusted friend. At a seminar I went to, we were tasked with sharing our vision with a complete stranger. Afterward, many people shared their experience with the whole group. For nearly every person, what seemed outrageous and impossible to achieve before they said it out loud became much more real and plausible after sharing it.

Through sharing our vision, we realize several things:

1. We're not the only ones with big dreams. Most people do have them, or did at one time; they're just afraid to share them with others.
2. Many times, the people with whom we share our vision would either like to help, or perhaps know someone who can help. Everyone wants to be a part of something big.
3. The more we share our vision, the clearer it becomes in our own mind. And clarity is essential to achieving dreams and goals.
4. Every time you share your vision, you reinforce your own subconscious belief that you can achieve it.

Living your life with a Sexy Little Twist includes knowing exactly what you want. Have you seen the movie *The Thomas Crown Affair* with Pierce Brosnan? Brosnan plays the title role of Thomas Crown, a wealthy entrepreneur who always knows *exactly* what he wants and goes after it with passion. Very sexy. Just saying.

The same is true in real life. Knowing exactly what we want gives us an air of confidence, certainty, and determination. It opens our mind to the infinite ways that we can get what we want. It affects our energy, which in turn has a subtle, but real, effect on those around us.

In later chapters, we'll talk more about visualization and about specifics on what to do, the actions you'll learn to take. For now, read the vision you created in this chapter at least once a day. Continue to hone it, giving it more detail. As you read it, do your best to see it in your mind's eye.

Sexy Little Twists of Knowing What You Want

*   A vision is only effective if it's truly YOURS.
*   You can only get what you want if you know what that is.
*   Sharing your vision helps you get clear on what you want and also reinforces the belief that you can achieve it.
*   Knowing exactly what you want is sexy.

Girl Talk (or Journaling Exercises):

Share one area of your vision with the group by reading it from your journal. After each person shares, have the group give up to five minutes of feedback and suggestions. Go around the room until each person has shared.

Discuss as a group how it felt to share your vision. How did you feel before you shared it? How did you feel after you shared it? Brainstorm other people in your life that it might be beneficial to share your vision with.

Think of one person you know, or know of, who seems to know exactly what they want in any area of their life. How do they behave differently from those who don't know what they want? How might you emulate their behaviors to bring about change in your own life? Discuss as a group.

Share with the group one action that you could take, or one behavior you could change, that would bring you closer to living according to your vision.

Discuss how you will use the concepts in this chapter to elevate and improve your results and your life. Commit to one small change that you will make in your daily or weekly habits, and be prepared to discuss your experience at the next meeting.

Chapter 10

God Loves a Great Party, Too!

"I've learned to use meditation and relaxation to handle stress . . .
Just kidding, I'm on my third glass of wine."
—**Someecards.com Stevenhumour.com**

You have adopted, during the course of your life, some underlying guiding principles about your place in the universe and your deservingness of the life vision you just created. Potentially, this takes us straight back to Chapter 4 and our passion assassins. If you hold an underlying belief that you are somehow undeserving of the life you have envisioned, then you are back to square one.

Embracing your vision at the deepest level of your soul and your being means that you acknowledge, accept, and understand exactly how your faith supports you in achieving your vision. If you don't see how your chosen faith could possibly support you in what you want to achieve, you'll want to learn more about your faith. Virtually every faith known to humankind supports the idea of honoring the self in order to serve others. And this is how you should view your vision, as the giving of your best self to your family and friends, your community, your country, and the world. You are nurturing and sharing the divinity that's inside of you. It's all about love, and every form of spirituality supports that.

I find that, in my current stage of spirituality, the idea of God working through me resonates the best. By honoring our true nature (our soul), we stay aligned with God, love, universal spirit, creative source, or whatever your faith names that pure energy that connects us all.

Since your life vision was created from a state of love and gratitude and honor of your true nature, success in achieving it is most certainly in alignment with your spirituality. But let's take this concept of the spirituality of success a little bit deeper. I'm sure that intellectually you agree that your vision is in alignment with your spirituality, but we want to make sure you *feel it* and *know it* at a soul-deep level.

Any study of the connection between spirituality and success will inevitably lead you to Deepak Chopra's book *The Seven Spiritual Laws of Success: A Practical Guide to the Fulfillment of Your Dreams*. Chopra does an amazing job of describing the connection between success in life and spirituality. The *universal* nature of the laws Chopra defines also helps tie us all together, regardless of your particular faith.

This chapter will provide insight into how these laws apply to living life with a Sexy Little Twist. Keep your newly-defined life vision in mind as you absorb these concepts, and you'll find that any concerns about misalignment with your faith will disappear.

"The source of all creation is divinity; the process of creation is divinity in motion; and the object of creation is the physical universe."
—Deepak Chopra

The Law of Pure Potentiality

This law encapsulates the field of all possibilities, infinite creativity, and, therefore, pure joy. As you envision transforming your life, the whole universe of possibilities is open to you, and your RAS will now allow those possibilities into your awareness.

This law also acknowledges our connectedness to everything and everyone else in the universe. The more you experience your true nature, the closer you are to the field of pure potentiality, to love, to creative intelligence, to God. This is why you create your life vision from the standpoint of honoring the true calling of your soul.

Furthermore, to experience your true self means that your own inner spirit (or God within or through you) is your internal reference point, your compass. I'm not making a statement here about disregarding the dogmas, practices, laws, or guidelines of your particular faith. Rather, this law simply rejects the notion of using "external" situations, circumstances, people, or things as our reference point. It rejects the notion of needing the approval of others or control over the things around us.

When we experience the power of our true self (or God through us), there is no fear, no compulsion to control, no struggle for approval or external power.

The polar opposite is when our reference point is our ego. But ego is not who you really are. Ego needs approval and control. It lives in fear, where your true self, your soul, is immune to criticism and fearless in the face of any challenge. Your true self feels neither inferior nor superior to anyone. By acknowledging and honoring your true self, you are one with divinity and it shows. People and circumstances that support your desires are naturally drawn to you.

So, how do we access this energy field of true potentiality, our true self? Chopra suggests practicing silence, meditation, nonjudgment, and communing with nature.

Practicing Silence

Make a commitment to simply *be* during a certain portion of your day. Take a few moments out of your day and don't DO—don't speak, do laundry, watch television, listen to music, or read a book. When you experience silence, your inner dialogue shuts up.

Truthfully when you first attempt this, your internal dialogue probably will go crazy. You'll feel an intense need to *do* or *say* or *think* something, anything, and sometimes everything at once. But your mind will give up after a while, when it realizes that *you* (the self, the spirit, the one making the choices) are committed to the silence. Then your inner chatter will go quiet, and you will begin to experience the *stillness* of the field of pure potentiality.

> *"Be still, and know that I am God."*
> **—Psalm 46:10**

Meditation

An absence of activity is one thing, and certainly it is a step in the right direction in our busy, frantic lives. But to go deeper into the stillness to access divine intelligence is what meditation is all about. And I haven't yet discovered a better way to get my ego out of the way so that I can access my true nature (a nice, stout martini runs a close second). Maybe you don't currently meditate, and the idea seems a little "out there" to you. Maybe it conjures images of robed monks living in solitude on Tibetan mountaintops. If so, it might be helpful for you to frame it differently. Perhaps you pray, or you have daily devotionals. In this context, think of the act of praying as *talking* to God and the act of meditation as *listening* to God. This simple analogy was very helpful to me as I began to practice meditation.

Or perhaps it would make more sense to you if you think of it as accessing your subconscious. Meditation helps us quiet our conscious mind (which is usually concerned with what's happening on the outside) in order to hear what's beneath all that chatter. When we intentionally quiet the conscious mind, what's left is our inner peaceful place.

No Judgment

Judgment is the constant evaluation of things, situations, and people as right or wrong, good or bad. When we constantly evaluate, classify, label, and analyze, we create turbulence in our internal dialogue. This turbulence constricts the flow of energy between us and the field of pure potentiality. It's quite human to judge (it's the foundation of survival), so perfection in this area is an ideal, rather than a reality. However, being aware of your judgmental thoughts, especially the judgment of others, can help you minimize them. This will tame your inner chatter to a level where your own true nature can be heard.

Communing with Nature

Spending time in nature also can help quiet your inner chatter and access your inner peace, if you'll let it. And I say *if* because many times when I go for a walk, my undisciplined mind will leap on the opportunity to hound me with all manner of scattered thoughts—to-do lists, unresolved problems, worries over future events that may or may not ever occur. If this happens to you, remember that *you* are in charge of your mind.

To summarize, the benefits of practicing silence, meditation, nonjudgment, and communing with nature are to get in touch with the innermost essence of your being. We can only live life with a Sexy Little Twist by completely understanding who that being is.

The Law of Giving

The Law of Giving, encouraged in some manner in every faith, also includes the equally important element of receiving, as there is a constant flow of energy in the universe. In order to keep the flow of energy moving, you must receive the gifts of the universe (God's gifts) and pass them on. Stopping this circulation of energy is like stopping the flow of blood to the body, or the flow of water in a stream. When blood stops flowing, it begins to clot; when water stops, it stagnates. This is why you must give and receive in an endless cycle in order keep success (or anything you desire) circulating in your life. This cycle of giving and receiving can easily be seen in healthy relationships.

In any area of your life, the more you give, the more you receive; because abundance is energy that constantly circulates. However, if you feel that you've lost something when you give, then you haven't truly given and the cycle hasn't been completed.

You see, your intention in giving is the most important component. If your intention is to create happiness for both parties (giver and receiver), and it is done unconditionally and from the heart, then you create an increase of abundance for both. Your frame of mind must be joyful in the very act of giving. When this occurs, the energy of abundance increases.

Putting this law into practice is easily summed up—whatever you want in your life, you must give unconditionally to others. Review the life vision that you created in the last chapter. If you've envisioned yourself experiencing more joy, then give joy to others. If you want love, then give love. If you want to be appreciated, then appreciate others. If you want material affluence, then help others to achieve material affluence.

Learn to wish upon others the blessings, good fortune, and good health that you desire in your life. Remember when we talked about the power of thought in Chapter 2 and how thoughts have an energy vibration? Even the *thought* of giving has the power to affect others.

The easiest way to start this cycle is to give something to someone. It can be as simple as a compliment, a smile, a silent prayer or wish, appreciation, a kiss, or even simply your attention. These nonmaterial gifts are quite powerful. The more you give, the more you will see the miracles of this law.

At the same time, make a decision to receive all that you're being offered. Accept compliments graciously; return that smile you've received. Enjoy the abundance of life around you in the form of sunlight on your face, a child's giggle, the song of a bird, or an appliance that works when you push the start button.

Make a commitment to keep abundance circulating in this manner by giving and receiving, giving more and receiving more. And remember that the most precious gifts are caring, appreciation, and love. Give and receive these the most.

The Law of Cause and Effect

Many Eastern faiths refer to this as "karma," but practitioners of other faiths will recognize the concept of "reaping what you sow." In this universal law, every action generates a force of energy that returns to us in like measure. If you want to create happiness in your life, you must learn to sow the seeds of happiness. In this manner, karma, or cause and effect, implies the importance of conscious choice making.

At any and every given moment, we have an infinite number of choices available to us. As we discussed in Chapter 6, some choices are made consciously, others not so much. The first and best way to maximize the use of the Law of Cause and Effect is to become consciously aware of the choices we make in every moment.

Remember in Chapter 6 where I admitted to subconsciously choosing to be insulted by a boy who made a face when he saw me? This is precisely the kind of subconscious choice that the Law of Cause and Effect points out. I actually made the choice to feel insulted, and I consequently experienced the effect of believing that I was ugly. It was a conditioned response, because I was unaware at the time of another choice. And this is where your power enters the scene of cause and effect. Where you remain aware and conscious of the choices before you, you will make decisions (the cause) that bring about better results in your life (the effect).

Allow me a few words about the lingering effects of bad choices made in the past (past karma) and the influence on your current situation. As we discussed in Chapter 3, you effectively transform your past bad choices by acknowledging them, asking yourself what you can learn from them, and, through finding that seed of opportunity for growth, connecting those learning experiences to your life purpose. In taking these steps, you convert your bad choices into positive experiences. As long as you continue to evolve in this manner, then the outcome ultimately will be happiness and success.

The Law of Least Effort

This is the law of harmony and love, which again resonates with every known faith. What is commonly called a "miracle" is an expression of the Law of Least Effort.

Least effort is expended when your actions are motivated by love, because nature is held together by the energy of love. When you try to control others, you waste energy. When you try to acquire things for the sake of ego, you spend energy chasing the illusion of happiness, rather than enjoying happiness in the moment. When you seek success for personal gain only, ignoring the element of serving others, you cut off the flow of energy to yourself. But when your actions are motivated by love, no energy is wasted. In fact, the energy generated by harmonious and loving action multiplies and accumulates; it then can then be channeled to create anything you want.

Here's the beauty of this universal law as it pertains to transforming your life with a Sexy Little Twist! Realize that if you develop your life vision from a place of harmony and love, through the deepest longing of your soul (your true self), then creation of your best life will require far less effort than it has taken you to create the aspects of your life that you don't want!

Put another way, the current undesirable aspects of your life are out of alignment with your true nature, your true self (we know this simply because they are undesirable to you). Therefore, creating these aspects of your life has actually required *more* effort to achieve than would have been required to achieve the life you desire. You've simply strayed from your true self. The good news is that now that you've consciously chosen the life you want, and you know you can consciously choose to stay in alignment with your true self and not your ego, it will require less effort to follow your true, desired path than to keep struggling in the same direction you're heading now. How cool is that?

So, there are three components to the Law of Least Effort—acceptance, responsibility, and defenselessness.

Acceptance simply means stopping the struggle against the present moment. Accept things the way they are now, rather than wishing things were different in your current situation. Here's the distinction: It's okay to *wish* for things to be different in the future; but in *this* moment, you must accept things as they are. In Chapter 5, we discussed how living responsibly toward reality was a component of Living Consciously, of high self-esteem. This means accepting the present as it is.

Responsibility is the next component of the Law of Least Effort, and, as we discussed in Chapter 6, this means that we avoid blaming others for our situation. Remember E + R = O? We acknowledge our own response as the only element that we have control over, and it is enough to entirely change the outcome of an event. Through responsibility, we turn every event into an opportunity for growth toward our true self, our path of least effort.

Defenselessness means that we let go of the need to convince or persuade others of our point of view. When you relinquish the need to be "right," you gain access to enormous amounts of energy that were previously being wasted. I can vouch for this one through my experience in my relationship with my husband. Early in our marriage, we would exhaust ourselves trying to convince each other that we each were "right." Letting go of this defense mechanism (that's all it really is) led the way to far more harmonious discussions, and, ironically, to the more frequent admission that one or both of us had a damn good point. Give up your defensiveness and realize how little your true self needs the protection anyway.

The Law of Intention and Desire

"Ask and it will be given you; seek and you will find;
knock and it will be opened to you."
—Matthew 7:7

Whether you consider the benevolent source of all good things to be God, or the universe, or a scientific process where your thoughts vibrate energy and information into physical manifestations of what you desire, it is universal to believe that there is power in asking for what we desire.

The two components involved in this cycle of asking and receiving are attention and intention. Attention energizes and intention transforms. Whatever you put your attention on will grow stronger in your life. Whatever you take your attention away from will wither, disintegrate, and disappear. Using the example of a romantic relationship, when you first meet, your attention is laser-focused on the other person, and the intimacy is unlike anything you've ever experienced. After some time of being together, you lose that focus. Your attention becomes spread out among all of your other priorities and obligations, which usually results in a lesser degree of intimacy in the relationship.

Attention is focus on what is, on the present moment. Intention is focused on the future, on what you want to bring about. So you accept the present and intend the future. The future can always be created through intention, but we should never struggle against the present.

The power of intention can be seen in practically every success story known to mankind. Even without the spiritual element, almost everything is accomplished through first setting an intention to do so. I'm leaving a little wiggle room here because of the many great discoveries that were made while someone was *intending* to do something else entirely (a la, the crunchy pretzel, which was the result of accidently over baking soft ones).

We'll discuss intention more in Chapter 12 where I'll show you how to develop affirmations for your goals and desires. But here are a few steps for putting this law into practice:

1. Again, meditate, preferably in silence. Get yourself away from ego and into your true self.
2. Maintain awareness of your true self, your true nature, as much as possible.
3. Let go of your attachment to the outcome. More on this in the next law.
4. Let God or the universe handle the details. Trust that the how will be arranged for you.

The Law of Detachment

This law tells us that in order to acquire or achieve anything, we have to let go of our attachment to it. Remember that saying, "If you love something, set it free"? This law is kind of like that. It says that we will never truly achieve or acquire anything that we obsessively cling to.

It does not mean that we give up the intention or desire of creating something in our life. We just give up our attachment to the specific result or outcome.

This is the part of achievement where our faith truly comes into play. In monotheistic faiths, we've heard the phrases "Let go and let God" and "Not my will, but yours be done." In other faiths, this is an acceptance that the universe will provide what we need and want. It also can be seen simply as a solid belief in the Law of Attraction—that what we ask for, if we believe, we'll eventually have.

Inherent in this law is the idea of faith and trust, the idea that we do not have to battle to achieve our heart's desire. If we sincerely have faith that what our true self desires will be delivered to us at the perfect time, then detachment is easy. In fact, if we believe that, then we're already detached.

The opposite of this state of trust and faith is attachment, which is based on fear and insecurity. This is the state of being terrified that we'll never achieve what we want to in life, never have the life we envision. Do you remember in the last chapter when I asked you not to worry about how you would achieve your vision, but rather just concentrate on the what? Worrying about "how" things will possibly be created is attachment. By focusing on the "what" and letting God or the universe or quantum physics take care of the details, we achieve detachment, trust, and faith.

This is not to say that we're not going to take action to create the life of our dreams. We're still going to have intentions, set goals, and take steps to achieve them. But between where you are now and where you want to be, there are infinite possibilities for how to get there. The fact is that when you're willing to embrace uncertainty (let go of your need for security), you may likely find something out there that excites you even more than your original vision. When you are open to new ideas and new opportunities (in other words, detached from your ultimate goal), you will be presented with all manner of amazing choices.

Chopra suggests the following steps to putting the Law of Detachment into effect:

Commit yourself to detachment. Allow yourself the freedom to be who you truly are. Avoid rigidly imposing your idea of how things should be. Avoid forcing solutions to problems and trust that the perfect solution will present itself at the perfect time.

Embrace uncertainty. Recognize that out of confusion, disorder, and chaos, solutions will emerge when you view uncertainty as an ally, rather than an enemy. True security and peace come from the wisdom of harnessing the opportunities provided by uncertainty.

Anticipate the excitement that can occur when you remain open to an infinity of choices. In this field of infinite possibilities lie the fun, adventure, magic, and mystery of life.

The Law of Purpose in Life

This is also called the Law of Dharma, from the Sanskrit word meaning "purpose in life." This law says that we are each put here to fulfill a purpose, and every known faith supports the idea. I won't delve into this topic too deeply here since we discussed this at length in Chapter 8. But it's worth pointing out that when you set about discerning the purpose of your life, you are performing a spiritual act.

As we discussed in Chapter 8, you have a unique talent and a special way of expressing it. There is something that you can do better than anyone else in the entire world. Furthermore, there is a need in the world that directly correlates with your specific gift. Where your unique talent collides with the world's unique need, sparks fly. Seriously. This is the point in our cosmos where abundance is created, both for you and those you serve by sharing your talent.

I get a little teary eyed at this point in my message, because it truly is the essence of a life well lived, a life of joy and abundance, for yourself and those around you. I can't stress enough how excited it makes me to think that even one reader would really *get* this message and consequently begin sharing their talent with the rest of us. The thought of that is awe-inspiring, to say the least.

But I digress.

Here again are the three components to the Law of Dharma or Life Purpose:

1. We're here to discover our true self, our own true nature, our higher self. We're spiritual beings in physical form, and we're here to honor that truth.
2. We're meant to express our unique talents. And, yes, we each have them.
3. Our talent must be used to serve humanity in order for us to completely fulfill the Law of Dharma. True abundance for all is achieved through the unique expression of your talent in the service of others.

Make the commitment to continue to explore and discover, or rediscover, your life purpose. Revisit the exercises in Chapter 8 as many times as you'd like in the pursuit of clarity. You'll thank me for it!

I hope that I've convinced you in this chapter that no matter what faith you practice, no matter what guidelines or dogmas or traditions your faith encourages or avoids, there are universal truths we can all get behind. On a spiritual level, we all are affected by the same laws in equal measure. And ultimately, we are all here to serve and help one another live our best lives. I love that I'm connected on a spiritual plane with every other Christian, Muslim, Jew, Buddhist, Hindu, Atheist, Agnostic, and person of every other faith out there. It warms my heart to know that connection is there, and it's very real.

My hope for you is that this chapter has quieted any doubts in your heart about the spirituality of pursuing your best life.

Sexy Little Twists of Spirituality

- Your vision is simply you giving your best self to the world.
- Practicing silence and meditation help us get in touch with our true self.
- If your vision includes receiving more love and joy, then give more love and joy. What you give comes back.
- Transforming your life to match the vision you created will take less effort than it took to create the life you have now.
- Discerning your life purpose is a spiritual act.

Girl Talk (or Journaling Exercises):

Discuss ways in which your current faith, or the one you grew up in, supports the idea of you achieving your dreams. Are there any ways in which you do not feel supported by your faith? If so, what are they and how could you go about rectifying that?

Consider the vision that you created in the last chapter. What are you wanting more of in any area of your life? Discuss ways that you could give more of what you want to receive.

Think of an area of your life that isn't currently working well for you. Share with the group the difficulties and struggles you've experienced. Discuss ways that living your vision for this area might actually require less effort, less struggle.

Share with the group your experience with meditation. What challenges does meditating present for you? What benefits have you experienced from it?

Do you think your life would be different if you meditated more frequently? If so, in what ways?

Discuss how you will use the concepts in this chapter to elevate and improve your results and your life. Commit to one small change that you will make in your daily or weekly habits and be prepared to discuss your experience at the next meeting.

Chapter 11

Your Gucci Bag List
(Buckets Have No Style)

"I desperately want to go camping this summer.
Preferably in a hotel. With a pool. And a spa."
—Anonymous

So, you know your life purpose and you've created your vision. The next step to life with a Sexy Little Twist is to set some goals based on what you now know you want to create in your life.

What's that? You've already made a goals list years ago (or months ago, or weeks ago), and nothing ever came of it? Excellent! Find it and dust it off! You're older and wiser now, even if it was last week when you created it. Past failure is absolutely no indication of future results! If it were, then nothing would ever have been, or ever will be, accomplished. Just because you didn't manage to make things happen before doesn't mean you won't now. You've got some new knowledge, some new tools and techniques, and you've got some new determination to make it happen.

If it's been a while since you looked at your list, then you may even find that some of your goals have been completed. Or you may find that some of the things you once thought were important no longer excite you. That's okay, too. Cross them off like you've accomplished them. You get kudos for acquiring the knowledge to realize that those goals won't make you happy or bring you fulfillment.

Whether you're starting with an old list or you're creating a new one from scratch, you'll have an exciting list of goals by the end of this chapter.

The Power of Goal Setting

Though you may have learned all of this before, let's review some of the theories around goal setting.

Setting goals accomplishes several things for us:

1. Sets our brain to work. We know that our brain is a problem-solving machine. When we give it a goal, our subconscious sets about trying to find the answer. This is where the "how" gets added to our "what."

2. Provides further clarity. By setting goals, our vision becomes clearer.

3. Helps us determine the actions we need to take. This is where the rubber meets the road, so to speak. We begin to break our vision down into more manageable tasks, actions that we can take to move toward what we want.

4. Challenges us to meet deadlines. When we set specific goals, we are committing to accomplish things by a certain date. This helps provide motivation. Compare this to the thought that you'll get around to doing something *someday*.

5. Boosts the odds of achieving them. Research has proven that having written goals actually increases your chances of achieving them. The simple act of writing your goals down on paper (or a computer) gives you an immediate advantage over just having them in your head. How easy is that?

So let's get started. This first exercise is called 101 Goals, and it's one of the most fun, exciting exercises you'll ever do. It's dream time again! Turn to a fresh page in your Sexy Little Twist journal and start fantasizing. What do you want to have, be, or do before you die? Where would you like to travel? What would you like to see? What would you like to learn to do? Are there classes you would like to take? A degree you'd like to finish? Where would you like to live? Would you like to own a second home somewhere? Are there people that you would like to meet? Are there events you would like to attend or participate in? Do you want to learn to play an instrument? Learn a new language? What are your fitness goals? Would you like to compete in a marathon or a bike race? What would you like to contribute? Who would you like to help? Just set your mind free and daydream like a kid.

A girl who goes to high school with my son was recently diagnosed with cancer and told that she doesn't have long to live. She made a bucket list that includes being serenaded, having a pie fight, and kissing Channing Tatum. Let her be an inspiration to you—they don't have to be big things, though some of them undoubtedly will be. Just think about what you'd regret not having done or tried.

Keep writing until you've listed 101 goals, or more. Don't worry if you actually have to spread the exercise out over several days. Just keep at it, and don't stop until you have more than 100 goals. Got 'em? Okay, we'll come back to this list.

Twist of Fate Goal

Our next exercise is to write a breakthrough goal, or what I like to call a Twist of Fate goal. A Twist of Fate goal is a goal that, once achieved, would become a life changer for you. It's a goal that would pick you up and set you on a new playing field. It's a goal that would require you to step up your level of action, commitment, and enthusiasm. It's a goal that would work wonders on your self-esteem, your belief in yourself, and your ability to accomplish anything you set out to do. It's a goal that, once achieved, could potentially have far-reaching consequences in your life, and the lives of others.

It might be something like the following:

- Publish a book.
- Get your master's or doctorate degree.
- Start your own business.
- Launch a website.
- Learn to speak another language.
- Compete in an Ironman triathlon.
- Get your pilot's license.

The idea is that it's a major accomplishment that would launch the remainder of your life in a positive direction. It could be seen as the turning point in living your life with a Sexy Little Twist.

It should be exciting and a little scary. Exciting because it fills you with enthusiasm and passion. Scary because it requires a major step outside of your comfort zone.

> *"You want to set a goal that is big enough that in the*
> *process of achieving it you become someone worth becoming."*
> —**Jim Rohn**, self-made millionaire, success coach, and philosopher

So give this some thought and come up with one Twist of Fate goal that you believe would completely change how you live the rest of your life. Write it down in your journal. Post it on your refrigerator or bathroom mirror. Set it up as your screen saver at work and at home.

Then, and most importantly, commit to the Rule of 5.

The Rule of 5 says that you take a minimum of five actions each and every day toward your Twist of Fate goal.

For example, if your Twist of Fate goal is to start your own business, then examples of an action might be:

- Make one phone call.
- Spend ten minutes researching the competition on the web.
- Write one page of your business proposal.
- Read one chapter of a book on the topic.

- Ask one person in your target market for feedback on your business idea.
- Open a checking account for your business.
- Think of a name for your business.
- Spend ten minutes on a brochure for your business.

I'm sure you can think of many other actions you could take, but you get the idea. This is how big things are accomplished—by taking small daily actions.

> *"A journey of a thousand miles begins with a single step."*
> **—Lao Tzu**

Small actions, taken daily over time, produce huge results. This is the method that Jack Canfield and Mark Victor Hansen used to make their *Chicken Soup for the Soul* book a bestseller. And it's the method I used to publish the book you're now holding in your hands. It works. And it works on any type of goal you want to accomplish.

Make Your Goals Pop!

Now that you've created your initial list and your Twist of Fate goal, there are some simple things you can do to further increase your chances of achieving them. So let's hone your list a bit more. I'm sharing this information with you *after* the goals exercise above, because it's important to create your initial list with a completely open mind. The best initial lists flow freely from a daydreaming state of mind. Trying to create the initial list while considering some guidelines would potentially hinder your ability to create a great list.

In her helpful book *Creating Your Best Life: The Ultimate Life List Guide*, Caroline Miller shares proven guidelines for increasing your chances of achieving goals. This book was based on the work of Edwin Locke and Gary Latham, two pioneers in the field of psychology.

Take some time to review your list of goals with the following guidelines in mind:

1. Make your goals challenging and specific. According to Gary Latham, this is the number one reason why people fail to achieve their goal. The goal must be specific enough to be measurable. Locke and Latham state, "That which cannot be measured cannot be achieved." Jack Canfield refers to this as the difference between a goal and a "good idea."

    Good idea: I want to get in shape.
    Goal: I will weigh 140 pounds by noon, December 1, 2016.
    Good idea: I want to improve my marriage.
    Goal: I will go on a date with my husband once a month beginning February 1, 2016.

    Being able to receive feedback on where we are relative to our goal enhances our success. If we're trying to save $1,000 by the end of the month, we can check each week that we've saved at least $250, or one-fourth of our goal.

    Locke and Latham also discovered that goals that don't challenge you don't get achieved. They must take you slightly out of your comfort zone in order to be motivating. This is contrary to what some people might encourage. You might hear that if you keep your goals easy, then you'll boost your self-esteem by achieving them. This isn't necessarily true. Our inner self knows the difference between achieving a low goal and a high one.

2. Set goals as an "approach" versus an "avoidance." Your goal should be stated as something that you want to achieve, rather than something you want to avoid.

    Avoidance goal: I want to stop eating junk food.
    Approach goal: Beginning August 1, 2014, I will eat three servings of
        fruit daily.

    The avoidance goal fills us with dread, while the approach goal causes us to look forward with anticipation. It also has been found that approach goals actually take up less energy, because avoiding something takes more mental and physical energy than approaching something.

3. Set goals that are "intrinsic" versus "extrinsic." Intrinsic goals are ones that we set because we have a passion for them. Extrinsic goals are the ones we set because of external pressure to do so. Many of us spend much of our lives without making a distinction between the goals we set for ourselves and the goals that we set because we think others expect them of us. If you really want to ensure and enjoy the pursuit of your goals and feel true pride in accomplishing them, then make sure they are *yours,* that they excite you at your core. If they do not, then it's possible that the goal is something you feel you "should" do. The "should" always indicates that someone else's expectation is present.

4. Keep your values in mind as you set your goals. Goals that are in alignment with your values and principles are more likely to be achieved, and once completed, are more likely to bring fulfillment. Think about your life purpose statement as you review your goals. Does each goal connect at some level with your overall purpose?

5. Make sure your goals align with one another. If you have goals that are in conflict, then the odds are that neither one will be achieved. In effect, you're battling against yourself. It would be difficult to achieve a goal of losing ten pounds while simultaneously trying to achieve a goal of taste testing every variety offered by The Cheesecake Factory. If you're passionate about both ideas, try prioritizing the achievement of one first, then the other. In this example, I'd recommend cheesecake first and then weight loss.

   However, I think you'll find that, for the most part, if you create your list from your own heart, your goals will naturally align with one another. My fitness goal of losing weight naturally aligned with my relationship goal of hiking Pike's Peak with my sons one summer. My personal goal of spending a weekend at a spa retreat naturally aligned with my relationship goal of enjoying a regular girls' weekend with my friend Laura. You'll discover lots of synergies like this in your list as well.

6. Create accountability for your goals. When you write down a goal, you are making a commitment to yourself to accomplish it. I can't stress enough how important it is to your self-esteem to follow through once

you've set a deadline. In his book *The Speed of Trust*, Stephen M.R. Covey states that to build trust with others, we must first start with ourselves. At the core of self-esteem is our own credibility with ourselves. Refer back to the vital practice of personal integrity that we discussed in Chapter 5. We may think that if we fail to follow through on a commitment that we made only to ourselves, then no one is hurt. In fact, we're hurting the only one who matters.

Do yourself a favor and take your commitments to yourself as seriously as you do your commitments to others.

To boost your odds of achieving your goals even more, share them with a trusted friend. Find someone who will help you be accountable for taking action. If you really want to make it happen, post your goal on your blog or Facebook page and report back on your progress each week. Talk about accountability!

The next step in living life with a Sexy Little Twist is to narrow our focus. It's no secret and no myth that as women we're able to multitask. But we've all experienced the effects of spreading ourselves too thin and trying to do too many things at once. Too often, we end up *sucking* at everything. We recognize that if we were able to focus on just a handful of tasks or projects, then we'd perform much better, and perhaps even do an amazing job at something! That's the idea behind narrowing our focus on our goals list. While we eventually want to get to all of them, we know we can't do them all at one time. So we prioritize. We focus.

The first thing I want you to do is to go back over your list and categorize your goals into the following life areas: Financial, Career, Relationship, Recreation, Fitness, Personal, and Contribution.

Don't worry too much if the goal can be considered in a number of categories. Just pick the category that comes to mind first.

Now, keeping in mind that your Twist of Fate goal should be included, I want you to pick one to three goals from each category that you feel are the highest priority in that life area. You can choose them based on the ones that excite you the most or the ones you feel should be done first or simply the easiest. However you choose will be fine, but be sure you have at least one from each category and be sure your Twist of Fate goal is one of them. These will be the goals that you work on first.

In the next chapter, I'll show you how to create and use affirmations. Affirmations not only will help you get rid of passion assassins (to move away from what you no longer want in your life), but also will aid in achieving your goals, to help you move toward what you do want.

Sexy Little Twists of Goal Setting

- Goals set our brain to work in achieving them, provide clarity, help us determine actions to take, and challenge us to meet deadlines.
- Twist of Fate goals are exciting and scary, and very sexy.
- Achieving a Twist of Fate goal is a life changer, working wonders on your self-esteem, your belief in yourself, and your ability to accomplish anything you set out to do.
- The Rule of 5, applied every day, is the surest way to achieve your Twist of Fate goal.

Girl Talk (or Journaling Exercises):

Spend some time discussing your 101 Goals lists with the group. Steal shamelessly if you hear exciting goals that you hadn't thought of. Discuss ways that you could collaborate to help each other reach your goals.

Share your Twist of Fate goal with the group. Is it a goal that you've just recently thought about, or is it something you've wanted to do for a long time? Explain why achieving this goal is so exciting and scary to you.

Share with the group what your top priority goals are and why. Discuss what your life would be like if you didn't achieve them, and what your life will be like when you do.

Discuss how you will use the Rule of 5 in the pursuit of achieving your Twist of Fate goal. What are some of the actions you will take each day? Commit to implementing the Rule of 5 in your daily habits and be prepared to discuss your experience at the next meeting.

Part III
Bringing It to Life (Yours)!

"The question isn't who's going to let me; it's who's going to stop me."
—**Ayn Rand**

Chapter 12

Your Very Own Double Secret Agents

"Think of your intention or goal as a fire. If you want to get the fire roaring, add fuel. The best way to do this is with high frequency feelings such as happiness, joy, love, and gratitude."
—**Starr Pilmore**

So, you've just committed all of your hopes and dreams to paper by creating a list of goals that you'd like to achieve, and you've narrowed that list so that you're using the power of focus to your advantage. What happens next?

You get doused in the face with a cold splash of doubt!

You start to get that sinking feeling as you hear the negative chatter erupt in your brain:

"I can't do that. I don't make enough money."

"If I were capable of doing that, I'd have done it already."

"My husband/children/parents/friends will never go for it."

"I'm too old."

"I'm too tired."

"I don't know the first thing about . . ."

"Only wealthy/lucky/smart/beautiful/talented people can do something like that. I'm not wealthy/lucky/smart/beautiful/talented."

And the mother of all negative chatter, "I don't have a moment of spare time."

Please be aware that these thoughts are perfectly normal, even for people who are already highly successful! This is your brain's natural protective response when presented with a new challenge. And you've just presented it with more than a hundred new challenges! So, don't panic. You're still in the right place, reading the right book. We're still together in this thing.

My husband and I talked for years about adopting a little girl. Adoption because we knew there were kids out there in need of a family (and truthfully I didn't relish the thought of another pregnancy), and a girl because we had three sons.

When we discussed the idea in earnest, we would come up with so many reasons as to why it wasn't a great idea that we'd end up doing nothing. It wasn't until I listened to an audio program by Dr. Wayne Dyer that I recognized these reasons for what they truly were—excuses. And more significantly, they were excuses that were robbing us of our dream of growing our family in the most beautiful, awe-inspiring way.

Excuses, Excuses . . . and How to Annihilate 'Em

In his program *Excuses Begone!: How to Change Lifelong, Self-Defeating Thinking Habits,* Dr. Dyer provides a fairly thorough catalog of the most common excuses we tell ourselves. He also debunks each of them with some practical tips and considerations. As we already know from Chapter 2, our beliefs can affect our physical reality. So it makes sense to confront these beliefs or excuses head on and determine if there's really any validity to them, or if they're just little "mind viruses" that we've picked up along the way. Do you recognize any of these as your own?

Excuse #1—It will be difficult. Do you really have empirical evidence that it will be hard to do? Dr. Dyer uses his own goal to quit smoking as an example.

Smoking requires the continual effort to ensure you have cigarettes on hand and a way to light them. It requires finding a place to smoke in our increasingly smoke-free world, dealing with the smell on your clothes, hair, and breath, and finding a place to dispose of ashes and butts, including emptying ashtrays. Smoking often is accompanied by a constant nagging feeling that one *should* quit, as well as the valid long-term effects on your health and the health of those around you. Is it truly more difficult to quit, or is it more difficult to smoke?

Excuse #2—It's going to be risky. If you're using this as a reason to avoid going after what you want, then consider for a moment what you're truly risking. What are you risking by playing it safe? It's a far greater risk to NOT be yourself, to reach the end of your life and feel like you wasted it.

Excuse #3—It will take a long time. Does it really matter how long it takes? How old will you be in five years if it takes you that long to achieve your goal? How old will you be in five years if you don't go after your goal? Time passes, regardless of whether we're living our dreams or not. Why not pass the time doing something you love?

Excuse #4—There will be family drama. Do you have the feeling that you *own* your children? That their lives are yours to control as you wish? Of course not! Consider for a moment that there is no one out there, your family included, who feels that your life is a possession of theirs. This excuse usually comes from a fear of criticism. It's likely that you'll gain far more respect than reproach when you live your own life.

Excuse #5—I don't deserve it. I'll refer you back to Chapter 5, as this excuse generally stems from a low self-esteem. Using this excuse provides us with protection from thoughts of "Maybe they're right. Maybe I am unworthy of happiness, success, love, etc." Make a note: You don't *earn* worthiness! You are equally as deserving as anyone else on this planet, including all the deliriously happy people.

Excuse #6—It's not my nature. I'll refer you back to Chapter 2 and our ability to change the very structure of our brains and our cells. If you've always been a certain way—overweight, unsuccessful, unhappy, broke, etc.—what a perfect reason to change that now! The truth is that only about 10 percent of your nature is hardwired; the other 90 percent is learned behavior.

Excuse #7—I can't afford it. Do you have an extra few thousand lying around in a bank account that you can spare right now? Maybe not. Are you fully capable of coming up with and executing a plan to achieve anything and everything on your list? Absolutely! Recognize and be grateful for everything in your life right now and more abundance will come to you.

Excuse #8—No one will help me. If you believe this, then your experience will match your belief. The truth is that there are lots of people out there who would love to help you achieve your dreams, because doing so helps them achieve theirs. A simple example—you want to build your dream home? There is someone out there whose purpose is to help others build their dream home. Trust that the right people will show up at the right time. And on a spiritual level, you're never truly alone in any worthy endeavor, because we're all connected.

Excuse #9—It's never happened before. This excuse comes from the belief that nothing ever really changes. But looking to your past to get an idea about your future is like driving forward while watching your rearview mirror. Everything that's ever happened in our entire human history was once something that had never been done. If there's something in your life that's never happened before, what a great time to make it happen now.

Excuse #10—I'm not strong enough. This is another excuse that keeps you locked in the past. If you believe that your true nature is weak, then you'll return to this thought to explain setbacks. If you'll dig deep into your subconscious, then you'll find another thought that supports the mind, heart, and soul as the source of your true power. Free of any ego-driven goals, the authentic self cannot be weak.

Excuse #11—I'm not smart enough. Your intelligence is so vast and so limitless that it cannot possibly be measured by an IQ test, or any other test. I'm quite serious. Are you necessarily a math whiz or a brilliant artist? Maybe not. But you're a genius, nonetheless. If you don't yet see it, trust that as you uncover your true self, it will be revealed to you. As Ethel Waters said, "God doesn't make junk."

Excuse #12—I'm too old or not old enough. According to whom? We all heard "You're too young for that" a lot as we were growing up. And then at some point it changed to "You're too old for that." Many times, it was our own inner critic that was doing the talking. Realize that nothing about your age should keep you from pursuing your dreams. You're the perfect age, right now.

Excuse #13—The rules won't let me. Be aware of "shoulds" and "shouldn'ts" in your thinking and your speech if you use this as a reason to avoid pursuing your dreams. Sometimes we create rules for ourselves that don't really exist, as in "My home should be spotless when my mother comes to visit." Also, I am not encouraging a disregard for the law, but recognize that some of the most horrible acts in history were performed under its protection. Oskar Schindler's idea to save Jews during the Holocaust was inspired by love; the rules at the time were not.

Excuse #14—It's too big. Contrary to popular belief, success at anything, especially anything really big, requires small thinking and small actions. If something feels too big to accomplish, then you're still looking at the gap between where you are now and where you want to be. Don't worry about the forty-eighth step; just take the first one.

Excuse #15—I don't have the energy. How many times a day do you hear someone say, "I'm exhausted" or "I'm worn out"? How many times a day do you say it? Low energy is a state of mind, and I'll prove it. Imagine flopping yourself onto your couch after a long, frustrating day at work and grabbing for the remote. Nothing's going to get you off that couch for at least two hours. Suddenly, your spouse bursts through the door, shouting that he's just scratched off a $50,000 winning lottery ticket! Did you get off the couch? You bet your ass, you did! Low energy is nothing more than a learned response, a lack of knowledge (or desire) about how to overcome our own inertia. In Chapter 13, we'll explore this topic in detail. For now, just remember that having high energy is a choice, and it's infectious.

Excuse #16—It's my personal family history. There are facts about our history that we cannot change. Our birth order; having siblings or being an only child; having married, single, or divorced parents; being adopted; our race or ethnicity; functional or dysfunctional families; good or poor health. Realize now that your relatives did the best job that they could, given their own strengths and weaknesses. You may not have been able to make peace with it as a child, but nothing's stopping you from doing so now. Be grateful for the life lessons you have learned. Did you have an alcoholic parent? Realize that it taught you the importance of staying sober. Like Excuse #9 above, this thought keeps you stuck in your past, driving forward with your eyes glued to the rearview mirror.

Excuse #17—I'm too busy. Probably the most popular one in today's culture, this excuse will eventually find you thinking "I've been working my tail off; why don't I have everything I ever dreamed of?" Because you're not working on the right things, that's why! Realize that you've chosen to prioritize your life the way it is, and therefore, you can choose to change it. Do you feel the need to say yes to every request made of you by your kids, your boss, your friends, or members of your church or other organization? Well, knock it off! Remember that you have a purpose to fulfill and everyone around you is best served by you doing just that.

Excuse #18—I'm too scared. Let's face it—we're all afraid of something. Success, failure, disapproval, poverty, getting old, public speaking, or my own personal favorites—infinity and eternity (creepy!). But seriously, fear is another mind virus that you've contracted along the way, for which the only antidote is love. Any spiritual guru, priest, pastor, or rabbi will confirm that fear is nothing more and nothing less than an absence of love. Infuse your life purpose with love for those you'll serve by living it out, and fear will dissipate on its own.

"Fear knocked at the door, love answered and no one was there."
—Anonymous

So, back to our story of adopting a little girl. We had heard that foreign adoptions were difficult (Excuse #1—too difficult) and expensive (Excuse #7—can't afford it). We also understood that adoptions took a really long time to complete (Excuse #3—it'll take a long time), and given that, just how old would we be when she graduated from high school (Excuse #12—we're too old)? And how would our families react (Excuse #4—family drama)? Our sons were getting older and more self-sufficient; could we really go back to diapers and car seats (Excuse #15—no energy)? We were swamped with the boys' activities and building our business (Excuse #17—too busy). And more importantly, we weren't the "saintly" types who could adopt a child with special needs (Excuse

#6—not my nature). I'm sure there were more, but you get the idea. The excuses were many, well established, and commonly known.

As it turns out, they also all were completely untrue.

Our daughter was dropped off at our hotel room in China on October 31, 2011, and we never looked back. That is, until I wrote these words.

Looking over the draft of this with my husband, we marveled at the puniness of those concerns compared with the joy we experience having her in our life.

Regarding Excuses #1, #7, and #17, no difficulty or expense or time commitment could ever make it not worth it. Our experience and maturity make us far better parents than we were for our oldest son (poor guy!), so Excuse #12 is moot. Our extended families adore her and dote on her almost as much as her big brothers do (I pity any young man who wants to take her out on a date when she's older!), so Excuse #4 never materialized. For now, she's still in a car seat, which she buckles herself into (no sweat); but we're already out of the diaper phase (I'm not gonna lie, I'm pretty freakin' psyched about this), so Excuse #15 just isn't an issue. And guess what? Regarding Excuse #6, not a single form that we had to fill out during our year-long dossier process asked if we were saints. Good thing, too, since you're really not supposed to lie on those things. Guess it just wasn't a requirement after all.

So let's take all of the negative, disempowering energy of our excuses and limiting beliefs and turn them around to help boost us out of our self-defeating thoughts into our brighter future. Remember that all of those limiting beliefs and excuses are nothing but chains and duct tape binding our authentic, vibrant, fun, joyful selves, and keeping us from actively pursuing our dreams. One of the most effective and widely-used techniques for overriding negative beliefs is affirmations. I want you to think of affirmations as Double Secret Agents (DSAs). You'll send DSAs into your psyche to sneak up on your passion assassins and eliminate them, before they have a chance to kill your dream life.

The best way to get rid of a passion assassin is to prove it wrong by doing the very thing you subconsciously believe you can't do. But sometimes, that takes a while, especially if it's a big goal. An affirmation or DSA is a tool to use in the interim while you're still moving toward a goal or a state of mind. A DSA is simply a statement that describes a goal in its already-completed state. There are two distinct uses for DSAs —attitude enhancement and goal achievement.

When used for *attitude enhancement*, DSAs can replace a previously-held mind virus, excuse, or passion assassin. When you become aware of a passion assassin, you can replace it by affirming to yourself that the opposite is true. By introducing this new way of thinking into your brain and repeating it often, you can eradicate the old belief and install a new, empowering one. Much like upgrading software on your computer.

When used for *goal achievement*, DSAs state your future goal as if it's already been accomplished, which creates something called "structural tension" in your brain. As I mentioned previously, stating and imagining your goal as if it's already completed causes your brain to go to work trying to close the gap between your dream and your physical reality. Your mind creates the "how" to achieve the "what."

Attitude Enhancement

So let's first look at using DSAs for attitude enhancement. When you become aware that you're having a negative thought or excuse, you simply replace that thought with a more empowering statement, as if you already hold the new belief. This new, empowering statement becomes the affirmation or DSA that you repeat to yourself, or out loud if you prefer. Short-circuiting the negative belief enough times in this manner will help you to adopt and assimilate the empowering belief, replacing the old one. You may have heard this referred to as a "mantra."

Here are Dr. Dyer's suggested affirmations for the list of excuses provided above. Feel free to use these or develop some of your own that resonate with you.

Excuse #1: When you find yourself thinking that something will be difficult . . .

DSA: I have the ability to accomplish any task I set my mind to with ease and comfort.

Excuse #2: When you find yourself thinking that going after your goal will be risky . . .

DSA: Being myself involves no risk. It is my ultimate truth, and I live it fearlessly.

Excuse #3: When you realize you're focusing on how long something will take to achieve . . .

DSA: I have infinite patience when it comes to fulfilling my destiny.

Excuse #4: When you are worrying that your actions will cause a family drama . . .

DSA: I would rather be loathed for who I am than loved for who I am not.

Excuse #5: When you catch yourself thinking that you don't deserve to be successful, happy, wealthy, etc . . .

DSA: I am a divine creation, a piece of God; therefore, I cannot be undeserving.

Excuse #6: When you find yourself doubting that it's in your nature to accomplish something or take an action . . .

DSA: My essential nature is perfect and faultless. It is to this nature that I return.

Excuse #7: When you have thoughts that you can't afford to have what you truly desire . . .

DSA: I am connected to an unlimited source of abundance.

Excuse #8: When you are fearful that you'll have to do it all by yourself . . .

DSA: The right circumstances and the right people are already here and will show up on time.

Excuse #9: When you doubt your ability to accomplish now what you've never been able to accomplish in the past . . .

DSA: I am willing to attract all that I desire beginning here and now.

Excuse #10: When you doubt or wonder if you're strong enough to do something . . .

DSA: I have access to unlimited assistance. My strength comes from my connection to my source of being.

Excuse #11: When you think that you're not smart enough . . .

DSA: I am a creation of the divine mind. All is perfect, and I am a genius in my own right.

Excuse #12: When you're plagued by thoughts of being too young or too old . . .

DSA: I am an infinite being. The age of my body has no bearing on what I do or who I am.

Excuse #13: When it seems that there are rules that keep you from achieving your dreams . . .

DSA: I live my life according to divine rules.

Excuse #14: When you're overwhelmed with how large a project or goal seems . . .

DSA: I think only about what I can do now.

Excuse #15: When you feel that you don't have the energy to live the life you want . . .

DSA: I feel passionately about my life, and this passion fills me with excitement and energy.

Excuse #16: When you feel resentment or regret over anything in your past . . .

DSA: I live in the present moment by being grateful for all of my life experiences as a child.

Excuse #17: When you just don't think you can squeeze one more activity into your busy schedule . . .

DSA: As I unclutter my life, I free myself to answer the callings of my soul.

Excuse #18: When you're afraid . . .

DSA: I can accomplish anything I put my mind to because I know that I am never alone.

Look at every excuse as a passion assassin. Your job is to catch those passion assassins in the act and rehabilitate them into productive, contributing citizens of your own inner society. Now that you have a catalog of helpful, empowering DSAs, develop the habit of interrupting those negative thoughts and reframing them into a more empowering dialogue. The more you do this, the quicker your positive results will show up.

Silence the Skeptic

When you state the new affirmation or DSA, does your brain immediately say, "Yeah, right"? If you're struggling with the idea that it could possibly be this simple—that lifelong thought patterns can just be replaced by new beliefs at will—I want to offer another, more in-depth affirmation technique.

In her book *Belief Re-patterning*, Suze Casey outlines a six-step process for turning limiting beliefs into empowering ones. Casey states that, for many people, jumping from a disempowering belief straight to an empowering one is too much of a leap. She says that the brain requires that some interim steps be taken, in order for the new belief to be credible. Much like stepping stones across a creek help us to get to the other side, the steps in Casey's Belief Re-patterning process help us to move from a lifelong passion assassin to a new empowering belief.

You can work through these thoughts and actions mentally, or for even better results, on paper. Here are the steps:

1. Forgiveness—Your inner coach enters the scene and encourages you to move forward. This is the point where you acknowledge where you are. Forgiveness statements are about letting go of the blame or shame that has kept you in the old belief. They are about initiating the process of change. Example: I forgive myself for believing that I'm not smart enough or talented enough to write and publish a book.

2. Permission—This step involves becoming observant of your inner critic and stepping out of your "stuck" place. You express the desire to take a step into new possibilities. There is a willingness to explore new positive options, and you invite yourself to move into something different. The energy around permission is feeling as if you *want to*, even if you aren't sure *how to*. Example: I give myself permission to stop feeling stupid and untalented and start feeling smart and gifted.

3. Choice—In this step, you place the limiting, disempowering, or negative belief (passion assassin) next to the empowering, positive belief. Your inner critic and inner coach are talking to each other, examining the differences and making a conscious decision. As you enter this stage, the feeling is that of being on the fence, balancing between the two options. Then the tipping point occurs, so that the decision is made. If you haven't yet moved into action but feel as if you *can*, you are ready

for the choice stage. Example: I know how it feels to be stupid and untalented, and I know how it feels to be smart and gifted. I choose smart and gifted.

4. Freedom—In this step, you begin to feel excitement. Your inner coach is stretching its wings and trying on the new feeling. You experience all the excitement of "*I get to.*" Your conscious mind is playing with the new, empowering belief and imagining what it will create. This stage is about projecting that empowering belief or feeling into the future and envisioning the actions you'll take to create it. Example: I am free to create smart and talented beliefs and feelings in my life.

5. Affirmation—Casey uses the term "affirmation" in a slightly different way. Rather than simply a positive statement that describes a new reality, the affirmation step of Belief Re-patterning acknowledges where you have experienced the empowering belief in the past and connects the new belief to specific, known experiences. Here you dig into your memory to find evidence that reinforces and expands your new, empowering belief, in order to attract more of the same. You anchor the new belief with observations like "Oh, sure, I've done that before," or "It's like that time when I . . ." Your inner coach brings concrete examples from your past to your conscious awareness. Example: I felt smart and talented when I got an "A" on that essay in high school.

6. Surrender—In this stage, you have arrived solidly at empowering, positive energy and belief, and you begin to define yourself in this way. The energy is that of being grounded, and you are actively creating the new belief as your way of being. You hear yourself say, "I am . . ." and you believe it! The energy of the new belief and emotion support you in consciously creating your life and moving forward in a purposeful way. Example: I define myself as smart and talented from now on.

So, for many people, simply developing a new affirmation and reading it regularly, while *feeling the feelings of having achieved it,* is enough to instill a new belief pattern. If, however, this method isn't working for you or you feel overwhelming disbelief when you state your affirmations, then try Casey's method of easing yourself into a new belief, one step at a time.

Goal Achievement Made Easier

We've looked at how to use affirmations for attitude enhancement. Now let's use them to boost our goal-achieving capabilities.

Remember that DSAs are a way of changing your negative self-talk (your inner critic) to positive self-encouragement (your inner coach). With DSAs, we also can bombard our subconscious mind with new thoughts and images of all our goals already complete. Where attitude enhancement DSAs help us eliminate existing disempowering thoughts, goal achievement DSAs help us quickly narrow the gap between what we currently have in our life and what we want in our life. It helps us move quickly from where we are now to where we want to be.

In goal achievement DSAs, we state our goals as if they have already been achieved. In his book *The Success Principles*, Jack Canfield (can you tell I dig this guy?) provides some fantastic, easy-to-follow guidelines for creating affirmations:

1. Begin your DSAs with the words *"I am."* Our subconscious interprets any sentence that starts with the words *I am* as a command—a directive to make it happen.

2. Use the present tense. Describe what you want as though you already have it, as though it is already accomplished.

    No: I am going to finish a triathlon.

    Yes: I am ecstatically crossing the finish line in a triathlon.

3. State it in the positive. Affirm what you want, not what you don't want. The unconscious mind thinks in images, so the words "Don't wreck the car" evoke an image of a car wreck. The phrase "I am no longer dating lowlifes" might evoke an image of paying for your own meal *and his* at a roadside taco stand.

    No: I am no longer dating lowlifes.

    Yes: I am enjoying dating grown-up men who treat me with respect.

4. Keep it brief. Think of your DSA as an advertising jingle or tagline. Pretend each word costs $1,000. Make it short and memorable enough to be recalled easily.

5. Make it specific. Vague DSAs produce vague results.

   No: I am driving my new car.

   Yes: I am driving my new red convertible 2016 Chevrolet Camaro.

6. Include an action word ending with *–ing.* The active verb adds power to the effect by evoking an image of doing it right now.

   No: I express myself openly and honestly.

   Yes: I am confidently expressing myself openly and honestly.

7. Include at least one dynamic emotion or feeling word. Include the emotional state you would be in if you had already achieved the goal. Some commonly used words are *enjoying, joyfully, happily, celebrating, proudly, calmly, peacefully, delighted, ecstatically, enthusiastic, lovingly, secure, serenely, passionately,* and *triumphantly.*

   No: I am maintaining my perfect body weight of 138 pounds.

   Yes: I am feeling agile and great at 138!

   Note that the last rings like an advertising jingle. The subconscious loves rhythm and rhymes. It's why we still recall "*I* before *e* except after *c,* and when sounded like *a* as in *neighbor* and *weigh.*"

8. Make DSAs for yourself, not others. Be sure your affirmations describe your behavior, not the behavior of others.

   No: I am watching Johnny clean up his room.

   Yes: I am effectively communicating my needs and desires to Johnny.

9. Add *or something better.* When you are affirming getting a specific situation (job, opportunity, vacation), material object (house, car, boat), or relationship (husband, child, friend), always add the words "or something (someone) better." Sometimes our criteria for what we want come from our limited experience. Sometimes there is someone or something even better available for us than we can imagine right now, so let your affirmations include this phrase when it is appropriate.

Repeating DSAs on a regular basis is a good and worthwhile effort, but the real magic of using affirmations comes from really getting into the *feeling* of already having what you desire. Here are Canfield's steps, with a few of my own modifications, for creating your DSAs:

1. Visualize what you would like to create. See things exactly as you would like them to be. Place yourself inside the image and see things through your eyes.

   For example if your goal involves buying a specific car, imagine yourself sitting in the driver's seat, seeing your surroundings from inside the car, as if you were driving it. Picture the exact color of the hood as you look out the front windshield. Visualize the scenery, whether it's a winding country road on a sunny afternoon or that hot guy standing on the street corner watching you drive by.

2. Employ the rest of your senses as much as possible—sound, touch, taste, and scent. What would you be hearing and feeling if you had already achieved your vision? In our car example, that might be your favorite music coming from the sound system and the feel of the leather-wrapped steering wheel beneath your fingertips. And how about that new car smell? Even better, go down to the dealership, take a test drive, and anchor that memory into your brain.

3. Feel the emotion you want to feel when you have created what you want—the feeling of pride at having accomplished your goal, or the relief of knowing the engine will start every time you turn the key. Every time you repeat your affirmation, really get into the *feeling* of already having what you desire.

4. Describe what you're experiencing in a brief statement, including what you're feeling.

5. If necessary, edit your DSA so that it meets the above guidelines.

To put your DSAs to work for you, review them one to three times a day. Canfield suggests first thing in the morning, in the middle of the day to refocus yourself, and before going to bed. Read them out loud if you like. Close your eyes and visualize yourself as the affirmation describes, really feeling the emotions of it. The stronger the feelings, the more powerful the process.

This act of *visualizing* is a very powerful habit, which successful people employ to accelerate their results. Professional athletes have long used this technique to boost their efforts, but it works for any type of goal that you want to achieve.

Courtney Kirschbaum, a friend of mine, had a great desire to do a TED talk, which is a speech at one of a series of global conferences where people showcase their ideas for making the world a better place. She had someone take a picture of her standing in front of a huge TED sign and Photoshop a title of "Courtney Kirschbaum Speaking Live, June 19, 2014." With the help of that photo, Courtney visualized daily stepping onto the stage at a TEDx conference and rocking the house with her speech. The outcome? Courtney's actual speaking gig at TEDx Edmonton was June 7, 2014.

That's the power of visualization, and you can put it to work in your life right now, this moment.

It's also true that music can have a direct impact on emotions; so, I create a DSA slideshow with pictures that represent my goals, and I set it to music that inspires me and makes me feel good. It's quite easy to do using simple computer applications like iPhoto, adding music to photos (some from my own collection, some downloaded from the Internet). My current DSA slideshow is set to "Feeling Good," performed by Michael Bublé. Gets me pumped up every time I watch and listen to it.

So, let's do this thing. Pull out your list of top priority goals that you set in the previous chapter, including your Twist of Fate goal. Write a DSA for each one, using the guidelines above. Be sure to use "I am . . ." to start each one, and use *-ing* words that excite you. When you're finished, do one of the following:

1. Write each DSA on a 3x5 note card.
2. Type the DSAs into a note file on your smart phone.
3. Create a DSA slideshow on your computer.

If you really want to knock it out of the park, do all three. Then make a commitment to read them, or watch them, on a daily basis, at least once a day.

Remember to feel the feelings of having each goal accomplished as you read it. If you do this before bed each night, expect to wake up the next morning with ideas for how to make it happen.

Sexy Little Twists of Affirmation

- It's normal for doubt to bubble up right after we set goals. Just let these little bubbles do their thing; allow them to fizzle and evaporate into nothing.
- Much of what we believe to be true about success—you have to be rich, smart, etc.—are really just excuses, which can be eliminated from your life.
- A DSA is a great tool for locking in a new belief and for bringing our dreams to us quicker.
- Visualization is the powerhouse of achieving goals.
- A DSA for you:
  "As I transform my life, I am One. Sexy. Chick."

Girl Talk (or Journaling Exercises):

Think of a goal that you dreamed of accomplishing for a long time but never achieved. From the list of excuses above, determine which ones you used as a justification for not going after what you wanted. Share your experience with the group and get feedback on actions you could take now to complete that goal.

Choose one of the excuses listed above, particularly one that you feel hinders your progress, and create a DSA to counter it. Share your new DSA with the group and ask for feedback on how you might improve it. Discuss ways you might use your new affirmation to eliminate this excuse from your life.

Share three of the goal achievement DSAs you created in the exercise above. Describe any sights, sounds, smells, and tastes associated with it. Describe how you will feel and the emotions you will experience having achieved the goal. Get feedback from the group on how you might improve them.

Discuss how you will use the concepts in this chapter to elevate and improve your results and your life. Commit to reviewing your affirmations from the exercise above at least once per day and be prepared to discuss your experience at the next meeting.

Chapter 13

Bouncing the Party Crashers!

"I'm trying to be Fabulous today, but I'm exhausted
from being so freakin' Fabulous yesterday."
—Pinterest via **Kristin Blaylock**

"The number of hours in a day is fixed, but the quantity and quality
of energy available to us is not. It is our most precious resource."
—Jim Loehr

You've developed some exciting goals, a vision for your life that you're passionate about, and a life purpose that gives you a reason to get out of bed in the morning. And now you're wondering "Where the hell is the energy to do all of this going to come from?"

In transforming your life, even through small, incremental changes, energy is vital. Your attempt at a Sexy Little Twist will fizzle out quickly if you lack the energy to make it through the day, let alone the energy to go after your dreams with enthusiasm.

*"A vision statement, grounded in values that are meaningful
and compelling, creates a blueprint for how to invest our energy."*
—Jim Loehr

In their book *The Power of Full Engagement: Managing Energy, Not Time, Is the Key to High Performance and Personal Renewal,* authors Jim Loehr and Tony Schwartz reveal their discovery (made through years of coaching high performers) that being fully *engaged* is the key to a happy, productive, fulfilled life. As a society, we've focused on time management to get more done, when we really should be focusing on energy management.

Our energy capacity diminishes both with overuse and with underuse, so we need to find balance between energy expenditure and intermittent energy renewal. Too much energy expenditure without sufficient recovery leads to burnout and breakdown. Too much recovery without sufficient stress leads to atrophy and weakness.

Humans are guided by rhythmic patterns—our breath, brain waves, heart rates, blood pressure, hormone levels, and sleep cycles. So too, all of nature is guided by rhythms—the ebb and flow of waves, the rising and setting of the sun, and the activity and rest of all animals. Thus, it is perfectly natural for our energy levels to oscillate and flux throughout the day.

We can systematically increase our energy capacity, however. Much like an athlete, we build our energy capacity (whether physical, emotional, mental, or spiritual) by pushing ourselves beyond our normal limits and then allowing for brief periods of adequate renewal and rejuvenation. Just as an athlete improves their physical endurance by pushing past their normal limits and then recovering, building capacity in any area of energy requires that we're willing to move beyond our comfort zone temporarily in order to experience the rewards of growth.

We're going to look at all four areas of energy—physical, emotional, mental, and spiritual—as all are vital to showing up Fashionably Late to your own life.

Physical Energy

It probably goes without saying that physical energy is fundamental. It is the foundation upon which all other activities and energies rely. That's not to say that you couldn't still be functional without having that foundation of physical energy (most of us are walking billboards to that fact), but having physical energy makes maintaining the other energies that much easier.

As with other topics in this book, you can find tons of information—books, advice, blogs, etc.—on the subject of maintaining your physical energy, so I won't delve too deeply here. But for a high-level overview, a few areas to examine for energy-stealers in your life are sleep, nutrition, hydration, exercise, and habits.

Sleep

Let's face it; your schedule is full. You're trying to manage your career; keep track of your kids and their schedules; help your parents out; maintain your home, uphold your commitments in your community, church, and local charitable organizations; and still try to find time to squeeze in keeping up with friends and loved ones. You know enough now to have so much to offer to others, but what you're lacking is time. So you steal time from the activity where it seems to matter the least—sleep.

Unfortunately, while it may seem like this is the logical activity to cut back on (after all, who's going to complain?), it's the worst possible scenario for your body and mind.

Inadequate sleep causes much more chaos than simply low energy. It impairs your ability to think and make good choices in all areas of your life, from fitness and nutrition to work and relationships. It reduces your ability to handle stress and moderate your emotions. It compromises your immune system and damages your brain. And just like we can't exercise once a week and expect to have a toned body, we can't overdose on sleep on the weekend and expect to have energy all week long. It's kind of a daily requirement that way.

That's the bad news. Let's talk about the good stuff.

Adequate sleep has so many benefits that I'll be hard-pressed to list them all. But here are a few highlights that getting enough sleep provides us:

1. Boosts your energy. Been a while since you woke up feeling invigorated and ready for your day? This isn't the kind of morning you'll get from an overdose, like sleeping late on the weekend. This takes a regular routine of getting enough sleep as a rule, rather than an exception.

2. Repairs your body. Our bodies are stressed during the day from physical activity, UV rays, environmental pollutants, and germs. While we sleep, our body produces more protein—the building block for cells—which helps repair our body and boost our immune system.

3. Improves your mood. Adequate sleep improves our judgment, decreases agitation and frustration, and gives our mood a boost. Getting enough sleep can help us avoid anxiety and depression.

4. Improves your memory. Having trouble remembering things? Forgetting commitments, the location of your car keys, or just what the hell you went to the kitchen for? Before you start fearing Alzheimer's, try getting adequate sleep.

5. Reduces your stress. Sleep deprivation actually triggers the release of stress hormones in our body. Nice, huh? I know it can be a vicious cycle when it seems that stress is what keeps us up at night to begin with. But the reverse is also true. We can create an advantageous cycle that feeds itself as well.

6. Improves your health. Our bodies have natural mechanisms that counteract disease, such as diabetes, heart disease, hypertension, and obesity. These processes are enhanced while we sleep.

7. Manages your weight. Yep, studies show that we're more likely to be overweight if we get less than seven hours of sleep a night. Exhausted *and* chubby, how's that for a gut punch? Apparently, inadequate sleep disrupts our body's normal hormonal balance and increases our appetite. I can attest that when I'm particularly tired, I'll tend to choose fettuccine Alfredo over a green salad and fresh fruit. You know, comfort food.

8. Helps you live longer. Studies show that people who regularly get enough sleep live longer, healthier lives than those who don't.

So, how much sleep is enough? While requirements vary from person to person and can even change over the course of your life, studies show that somewhere between seven and nine hours a night is appropriate. And that doesn't mean you can add the hour and a half on the couch to the five hours you got between 1 and 6 AM. It means seven to nine *consecutive* hours. Without delving too deeply into it here, just trust me and the research. Getting eight total hours of *interrupted* sleep is not the same at all as eight hours of consecutive sleep.

And yes, I hear some of you saying, "Well, I'm just different. I can function perfectly well on five hours a night and have been for years." All I can say is, if you're functioning well on five hours a night, think how much of a rock star you'd be if you got the appropriate amount. Is it possible that you're having complications from it—colds that linger, relationships that falter, projects that go unfinished, decisions that go unmade, unwanted belly fat that won't respond to diet or crunches—and you're just not connecting the dots? Only you can say. I would suggest that you give adequate sleep a thirty-day trial and see if anything changes. It's well worth it to discover that you're more of a genius than you realized.

Nutrition

As with several of the other factors affecting our level of energy on a daily basis, nutrition is a topic that can and does fill entire libraries. My goal here is to give you some highlights on how reviving your nutrition habits can boost your Sexy Little Twist efforts.

Is it time for a pep talk with yourself about your diet? Are the foods and the amounts you're eating serving your health or detracting from it? Are you eating like the mature, successful, confident, sexy, centered person you want to be? Do you regularly choose food and amounts that boost your self-esteem and bring you closer to your goals, fitness or otherwise? If not, it might be time to reassess.

Do you eat consciously or do you eat out of habit, for the sake of expediency, or to assuage or evoke emotions?

It's no secret that certain foods contribute to healthy energy and others detract from it. Many of the foods we eat create fake energy—a brief, frantic burst that subsides into lethargy shortly thereafter.

It's a worthy project to assess your diet and commit to making some changes. As you begin to learn more about nutrition, you'll find that even small tweaks over time will have a huge impact on your energy level.

If you take nothing else away from this section of the book, please get this point: Your nutrition gets a Sexy Little Twist of momentum at the grocery store. That's where any changes in your eating habits really get a foothold. Making healthy eating choices on an ongoing basis is so much easier to do if you actually have healthy options to choose from at home.

In my journey to fitness, there were many leaps forward as well as setbacks. Making a leap forward was much more difficult to do when chips and cookies were all I could find in the pantry. Maybe the idea of not having any junk food on hand gives you night sweats; so if that's too much of a stretch, at least have the choice of some healthy foods on hand as well. And there are lots of choices for healthy foods available now, so I'm sure you'll find some you can get excited about. Browse your grocery or market aisles and try some new things. Just make sure that healthy options are represented at least as much as junk food in your cart.

Another Sexy Little Twist of nutrition that I adopted: I'm beyond the stage in life where I feel like I need to eat things I don't really care for. For example, for years when I packed a lunch, I always put American cheese on my sandwiches. A few years ago, as I was counting calories and really assessing everything I consumed on a daily basis, I realized I don't even like American cheese. I just always put it on my sandwiches out of habit. Because my husband and kids like it, I always have some in the fridge. So I stopped, and I found I was perfectly content eating sandwiches without it. On the rare occasions when I get a breakfast sandwich from a fast food restaurant, I ask them to leave the cheese off. When you examine what you're eating, you'll likely find that there are some calories you can eliminate without feeling a sense of loss.

In terms of energy, it's not only important to be aware of *what* you're eating; *when* you're eating also can have an impact.

You've already heard that eating breakfast is crucial to your health, including healthy energy throughout the day. But keeping your blood sugar levels regulated throughout the day also makes a huge difference. This can be accomplished through "grazing," or eating small amounts of healthy calories frequently throughout your day. A drop in blood sugar level causes a drop in your energy; this drop often presents itself as a hunger growl, which prompts you to grab the first available cookie.

You can easily avoid this blood sugar drop by nibbling on nuts, Greek yogurt, dried fruit, or any number of other healthy snacks at frequent intervals in your day. Ideally, you would munch on something between breakfast and lunch, again between lunch and dinner, and perhaps even between dinner and bedtime, depending on how late you eat dinner.

One more thing about nutrition and then I'll leave you alone about it: consider that your system might have a slight intolerance to certain food types. In *The Virgin Diet*, author J. J. Virgin outlines a plan for eliminating the seven most common high-intolerance food types and then adding them back to your diet one at a time. This helps to determine which, if any, of the foods you are eating cause problems for you, such as energy dips or extra weight that doesn't respond to exercise. The seven foods Virgin recommends investigating are dairy (including Greek yogurt), eggs, corn, peanuts, soy, gluten, and sugar. If you're following the other guidelines for maintaining physical energy and you're still wiped out, then you might think about checking into food intolerances.

Hydration

The very first potential culprit to examine if you're feeling fatigued or less than energetic is your daily water consumption. In her book *Energy Now: Small Steps to an Energetic Life*, Michelle Cederberg states that lack of water is the number one trigger for daytime fatigue. Even mild dehydration (as little as 1 or 2 percent of your body weight) can lead to fatigue, muscle weakness, and dizziness.

In addition to an energy boost, here are some of the other benefits of keeping yourself hydrated:

1. Helps you think more clearly. Our brains are made up of 75 percent water, which is essential in neurological transmissions. Drinking enough water each day helps you remain mentally alert and avoid difficulties with short-term memory and concentration.

2. Reduces the number of headaches. Since your brain's water content is so high, even slight dehydration can cause a mild headache. Before reaching for the aspirin or ibuprofen, try drinking a glass or two of water.

3. Helps regulate your temperature. You already know that your body cools itself by producing sweat and by evaporating water out of your pores. Drinking water keeps that cycle of fluid evaporation productive and healthy.

4. Helps with digestion. If you're suffering from constipation, again look to your water consumption as the first step in recovery. Adequate water is also key in helping your digestive system distribute nutrients from the foods you eat. If you're eating healthy anyway, might as well get the most out of what you eat by ensuring your body has enough water to make use of it.

5. Helps reduce the risk of disease. Every system in your body depends on water to function properly—your brain, your immune system, your joints, your digestive and respiratory systems, even your very cells. It's not difficult to understand that adequate water can help prevent serious breakdowns in your body.

6. Helps maintain a healthy back and joints. Adequate hydration has been shown to relieve back and joint pain for as many as 80 percent of sufferers.

7. Helps improve your complexion. The largest organ in your body is your skin. Keeping your body hydrated softens your skin, diminishes wrinkles, and tightens sagging skin. What's not to love?

8. Helps manage your weight. You probably won't find a conscientious weight loss program out there that doesn't at least mention the importance of hydration. Cederberg lists the following benefits of adequate hydration as it relates to losing weight:

   a. Drinking more water might encourage you to drink fewer high-calorie drinks.

   b. Our chronically dehydrated bodies send us signals that feel like hunger pangs when we really just need more water. Once you treat your body to the water it's craving, it will no longer confuse hunger and thirst, and you'll consume fewer unnecessary calories.

c. Water can act as an appetite suppressant. In a University of Washington study, one glass of water eliminated midnight hunger pangs for nearly 100 percent of the participating dieters.

d. Keeping yourself hydrated actually keeps your metabolism up. Even mild dehydration can slow your metabolism by as much as 3 percent. And as you probably already know, slowing your metabolism means your body will burn calories much more slowly than it should and potentially store extra calories as fat.

So, how much is enough? You'll get many answers if you take the time to research this question, but a good general guideline, and one that most experts can agree upon, is sixty-four ounces (two liters) a day.

Activity/Exercise

Exercise energizes us. I know it; you know it. The difficulty for so many of us is "finding" the time. Let's just get it out in the open right away—it's our responsibility to *make* the time. Give yourself "the look" anytime you catch yourself using the phrase "I can't find the time." There isn't any hidden pocket of time in our day that we're suddenly going to discover. It's always twenty-four hours and always has been—each day, every day. No exceptions.

So we're tasked not with *finding* the time to prioritize our health and fitness, but with *making* the time instead. And who's going to make the time? Not our spouse. Not our children. Not our friends or our boss. Not the fitness fairy either. That's right; we are!

Make the commitment today that you are going to honor your true self, your inner beauty, your soul within, by taking better care of the package it's currently housed in—your body. After all, who is going to take care of everyone and everything else in your life if you're not healthy?

As I mentioned above when we talked about getting adequate sleep, you may think you're handling everything just fine without exercising your body on a regular basis. That may be true. But just think about how amazingly productive, energetic, and centered you would be if you took the time each day to revitalize yourself.

If the idea of squeezing daily exercise into your schedule fills you with images of hungry kids, angry bosses, stacks of paperwork, dirty dishes, or even embarrassing workout clothes in a crowded gym (I'm convinced this is a more upsetting and more common dream than standing naked on a stage), then let's change how you're viewing daily exercise. Studies show that you can get some benefit from just a few minutes of exercise. Rather than try to find a two-hour period where you can drive to the gym, work out, and drive home (although this is a great option if you can swing it), why not try one or more of the following each day:

- Do a few stretches when you wake up in the morning.
- Put a hand weight in your laundry room and do a few tricep curls each time you're there.
- Contract your stomach muscles for thirty seconds at a time while you're driving. Relax. Repeat.
- Take the stairs at work.
- Instead of driving around trying to find a close spot, park at the back of the parking lot and walk.
- Do crunches while you're watching TV.
- Do jumping jacks or lunges while you're waiting for dinner to cook.
- Squeeze in a fifteen-minute walk before or after dinner.

The idea is to get you moving more and sitting still a little less. Any activity is better than none. Start small and you may find that it encourages you to do a little more.

If you're thinking that you don't have enough energy, remember that this is another cycle that gains momentum as you move in the right direction. If you can take a walk before or after dinner, rather than plopping yourself on the couch (which is what you'd rather do), then you'll likely sleep better that night, which will lead to a more energetic tomorrow. Then tomorrow, the walk will be just a bit easier to manage than it was yesterday.

Habits

Here are a few habits that have a tendency to steal our energy:

- Smoking.
- Drinking excessive amounts of alcohol.
- Watching violent or disturbing television before bed, which has the potential to inspire disturbing dreams that interrupt good sleep.
- Using the bedroom for anything other than sleep and sex which causes our brain to stay active when we climb into bed, rather than begin the process of winding down toward sleep.
- Using electronics just before bed. There's a new theory circulating among health experts that the blue light emitted from electronic devices may suppress your body's ability to secrete melatonin, which is a sleep hormone. Your options? Avoid the electronics or get yourself a pair of glasses with orange lenses that block the blue light.
- Not establishing good sleep preparation habits. Creating a bedtime routine teaches your body to properly wind down for sleep, which in turn helps sleep come more easily.

One more thing about physical energy—there are other health-related issues that cause physical fatigue. It's never a bad thing to check in with your doctor if you're having issues with maintaining energy.

Emotional Energy

Now let's explore the concept of emotional energy. While physical energy is the foundation, emotional energy actually makes up the lion's share of our overall energy supply. In *The Emotional Energy Factor*, author Mira Kirshenbaum shares that fully 70 percent of our total energy is emotional—the kind that manifests as hope, resilience, passion, fun, and enthusiasm.

Loehr and Schwartz share that performing at our best requires that we access pleasant and positive emotions: the experience of enjoyment, challenge, adventure, and opportunity. Any activity that's enjoyable, fulfilling, and affirming serves as a source of emotional renewal and recovery. Negative emotions, on the other hand, are costly in terms of energy expenditure and don't provide much benefit, except in extreme survival situations.

Kirshenbaum advises that the trick to making the most of emotional energy is to learn how to protect and replenish your reserves of the stuff. You do this by first learning to recognize what drains your energy—certain situations; toxic people; or poor mental habits like worry, guilt, indecision, and envy—and taking steps to avoid or minimize it. Then, you figure out what replenishes your energy—pleasure, prayer, novelty, anticipation, fun—and give yourself more of it.

Kirshenbaum makes a statement so critical to your new Sexy Little Twist that I'm quoting her directly here: "Everything worth doing that's difficult gets lost without emotional energy . . . Dreams die when we lack the emotional energy to hang in there in the face of all the obstacles."

Since we want your newly rediscovered dreams to flourish—now that you're back on track to living your life with a Sexy Little Twist—emotional energy to see them through to fruition is paramount. The great news? Emotional energy is a renewable resource! The more you live your life with a Sexy Little Twist, the more emotional energy you'll generate!

In the interest of recognizing what drains you and what you can do about it, here are what Kirshenbaum has found to be the eight most common emotional energy drains, along with how to counteract them:

1. Other people's expectations (OPEs). Are you living someone else's dream? If so, you're expending energy but starving emotionally. The counter? Declare your independence. You bought in to others' expectations in the first place; you can set yourself free. Continue to work through identifying your passion assassins as we discussed in Chapter 4 and eliminating them as we discussed in Chapter 12. Keep your intentions on your own vision through the regular review of your affirmations.

2. Loss of self. When you find yourself continually bending to what those around you prefer, even in the little things, you slowly check out of your own life. The solution: personalize your life. Ask yourself, "If it were up to me, what would I . . . hang on my wall? Wear to work? Do

for fun?" Make an effort to find more pockets of freedom where you can be more yourself.

3. Deprivation. Duties, tasks, and drudgery. Your life fills up with "shoulds" and "don'ts." You gain weight trying to get emotional energy from food. The fix—add pleasure, beauty, and fun. Pleasurable, satisfying experiences—both large and small—are really what you're craving. In setting your goals and developing your affirmations, you've planned for big treats to look forward to. Don't forget to work in the little things each day.

4. Envy. You may not always feel this directly, but you might find yourself feeling a bit depressed after hearing of someone else's good fortune. To counter this, count your blessings. As we discussed in Chapter 7, look at what you have and actively feel grateful. Comparison to anyone who's not you is a waste of energy. As Oscar Wilde said, "Be yourself; everyone else is already taken."

5. Worry. Worry simply torments and exhausts us without ever coming up with good ideas. The cure for this one is action. Do one thing that brings you closer to coping, even if that thing is getting out of the bed you weren't sleeping in anyway to make a list.

6. Unfinished business. Unmade decisions and postponed projects drain you. The solution? Do it or dump it. Forget about the perfect decision. Trust yourself and make a choice. If you can't find a good time to do something, examine it for OPEs. Maybe you can just cross it off the list without ever doing it.

7. Overcommitment. Do you have an overdeveloped "yes" muscle? Are you always saying "yes"—to your boss, mother, kids, friends; to requests, favors, and meetings? The simple solution is to use that "yes" muscle in service to yourself. Tell someone else "no" every once in a while just to feel your own power. Who knows, you may find a passion for it. If nothing else, you'll gain a whole new sense of your self-care abilities.

8. Holding on to loss. Fresh loss is urgent, but old losses you can't let go of are dead weight. Fix it by indulging in epic mourning. Take off from

work, stay in bed, and do nothing but cry until you're all cried out—and bored. Rewrite that story you're telling yourself in your head. Then go out and embrace your new Sexy Little Twist of a life.

Your exercise for this chapter is to pull out your Sexy Little Twist journal and spend three to five minutes on each of the following three areas:

1. Where do I need to personalize my life? Is my workspace decorated to my liking? Does my bedroom reflect my own tastes as much as my spouse's? Do I ever honor my own desires in the choice of restaurants or what to cook for dinner? Do I drive the kind of car that I want? Do I spend my free time doing things I love? Just spend three to five minutes exploring all the areas of your life where you might infuse a Little More YOU into your life.

2. What are some things that I could do to infuse beauty, passion, and fun into my life? What do I love to do? What would I love to learn? How would I love to spend my free time? Where would I love to go? What are some small things that I could do on a daily basis that would add pleasure to my day?

3. Where in my life do I need to learn to say "no" so that I have time to say "yes" to the things that really spark my passion? Who do I need to let down easily so that I can lift myself up, which is ultimately for the good of all? How might I avoid overcommitting to things that don't excite me so that I have time for the things that do?

While we're on the subject of emotional energy, it's worth mentioning that sometimes our lack of energy comes down to simple boredom. Are you enthusiastic about your daily activities, the food you eat, your exercise, your job, your relationships, and your hobbies? If not, then maybe you'll want to rethink some of these areas to see if you can infuse more passion into your day. Nothing energizes like passion.

I don't mean to suggest that we need to be bubbling over with excitement and enthusiasm every moment of every day. Wouldn't that be annoying? But a little added passion here and there can go a long way toward giving you an energy boost.

If your current workout feels like drudgery, try something new, like yoga or Pilates or Rumba. Switch it up with a dance class or lap swimming or any number of other options. Or set a goal to hike a nearby (or distant) peak and let the training for it infuse your current workout with new purpose.

Ever wanted to learn a new hobby or take up an old one? Take a few small steps in that direction and see how the enthusiasm of learning something new can spill over into your work.

Here's another weird way to increase your passion that I've experienced. Ever get bored with your food? Do you cycle through the same four or five meals for dinner each week? Bring basically the same thing for lunch every day? Grab the same easy, no-cook breakfast each morning? Try some new recipes or snacks.

Sometimes it's a simple matter of breaking out of our old routine that sets us on a higher emotional energy field.

Mental Energy

In his blog, Sebastian Marshall refers to mental energy as the ability to stay motivated and disciplined, to be highly productive and highly creative, and to feel vibrant and optimistic about the future. Loehr and Schwartz state that mental energy is used to organize our lives and focus our attention. It is the energy that encompasses the creative process. And the state of mental energy that serves us best is realistic optimism—seeing the world as it is but always working positively toward a desired outcome or solution.

All agree that using willpower, in any form and for any reason, expends resources from our pool of mental energy. When we use willpower, we are making a decision whether or not to override whatever action we would otherwise have taken. This is why good habits and rituals, based on what we value, are so important. When we do something out of habit, it eliminates the mental energy drain of trying to decide whether or not to do it.

In addition to building habits and routines based on what we value and want to achieve in our life, here are some additional suggestions from Marshall for keeping your mental energy high:

- Avoid temptation in the first place (an example I mentioned above is not purchasing junk food at the store; therefore, it's not on hand at home to tempt you).

- Make unimportant decisions quickly—trivial decisions are best made right away, even if it risks overlooking a slightly better alternative.

- Get out of bed soon after waking. Not only does this teach your body to transition properly from asleep to awake, but it also helps avoid depletion of mental energy (fighting the temptation to stay in bed) before you even get up in the morning.

- Focus on one complicated task at a time—switching back and forth requires more mental effort to refocus.

- Keep your blood sugar moderately high through eating small amounts frequently (glucose is the only fuel your brain uses) . . .

- But not *too* high. Too much sugar causes a rapid depletion as your body quickly stores excess sugar (causing you to experience a sugar crash).

- Avoid food that's difficult to digest since digestion then becomes your body's priority.

- Stay active as you work—it keeps your blood flowing, supplying your mind with a steady stream of fuel.

- Spend time only on activities that deserve your mental energy. Give yourself permission to dump unworthy mental clutter.

- Sleep at the same time every night, as it helps you sleep well.

- Write things down to free up your short-term memory. This is why to-do lists are so powerful—they save us from spending energy on trying to remember everything.

- Take breaks—real ones that require no conscious decisions. Take a shower, go for a walk, or meditate.

- For difficult decisions, write a short list of options and work from that. This allows your mind to focus quickly on choosing the best option, rather than expending energy trying to hold all of the options in memory.

- Be a little more extroverted—don't spend as much energy self-monitoring.

- Work and live in a comfortable environment since discomfort causes distraction.
- Choose to spend more time on activities that absorb your attention—a state of absorption referred to as "flow."

Other things that will support maintaining your mental energy are mental preparation, visualization (for example, reviewing your affirmations while you visualize having them completed), positive self-talk, creativity (and trusting the creations of your mind as discussed in Chapter 5), and learning something new (stretching your mental capacity).

Spiritual Energy

We discussed spirituality at great length in Chapter 10, but it's worth mentioning here that your spirituality has an energy that is expended and renewed, just like your other energy types. Your spiritual energy stems from your connection to a deeply held set of values and to a purpose beyond your own self-interest, i.e., your life purpose. While your quantity of energy is predominantly a physical issue, your motivation to spend it is a spiritual one.

The way to maintain your spiritual energy is by maintaining a balance between your commitment to others (a purpose beyond yourself, your life purpose) and adequate self-care. The capacity to live by our deepest values depends upon regularly renewing our spirit—seeking ways to rest and rejuvenate and reconnect with the values we find inspiring and meaningful. It's worth noting that the energy of the human spirit can and does override even the most severe limitations of physical energy.

Sexy Little Twists of Energy

- The key to maintaining energy—physical, emotional, mental, and spiritual—is to find a balance between energy expenditure and energy renewal.
- To build your energy capacity—whether physical, emotional, mental, or spiritual—push beyond your normal limits (moving outside of your comfort zone) and then allow rejuvenation.

- Areas to examine for achieving more physical energy are sleep, nutrition, hydration, and exercise.
- The secret to managing emotional energy is to recognize and minimize what drains it and allow yourself more of what replenishes it.
- Mental energy is drained through the use of willpower; creating automatic habits minimizes the use of willpower and preserves precious mental energy.

Girl Talk (or Journaling Exercises):

Spend three to five minutes writing in your Sexy Little Twist journal about your level of physical energy. Do you awake alert and ready to greet the day? Do you run out of steam after lunch or after work? Do you feel energized or lethargic most of the day? Share with the group one area—whether it's in sleep, nutrition, hydration, or exercise—where you do a great job. Share with the group one area where you could improve, including one small change you might make to increase your physical energy.

Review the list of the eight most common emotional drains above and share with the group one area that's been a challenge for you. Discuss with the group ways that you might avoid or minimize the problem in the future.

Think of an area in your life that has required great willpower to overcome. Share with the group ways that you have minimized (or will in the future) the willpower that's required. How might you create a ritual or habit that eliminates the need for willpower in this situation?

Discuss how you will use the concepts in this chapter to elevate and improve your results and your life. Commit to one small change that you will make in your daily or weekly habits and be prepared to discuss your experience at the next meeting.

Chapter 14

Does Your Party Have a Dress Code?

"Sex appeal is something that you feel deep down inside. It's suggested rather than shown. I'll admit that I'm not as well-stacked as Sophia Loren . . . but there is more to sex appeal than just measurements."
—Audrey Hepburn

"Beauty, to me, is about being comfortable in your own skin. That, or kick-ass red lipstick."
—Gwyneth Paltrow

Once upon a time in my youth, a few friends and I approached the entrance to a trendy bar in downtown Chicago.

Said the bouncer at the door to my friend Nick: "Sorry, buddy. We have a dress code; you can't come in here wearing jeans."

My friend Nick, without blinking an eye: "They're GUESS jeans."

Bouncer: "Come on in."

When this exact same verbal exchange took place later that night at yet another bar, I realized that it wasn't simply that Chicago bouncers had an appreciation for designer jeans (though that may have been true). What was really happening was that my friend Nick was expressing total confidence in how he looked. He was calmly asserting his *"inner knowing"* that his attire and appearance were more than enough.

Having made it this far in the book, you've recognized by now that being Sexy is predominantly about how you feel about yourself on the inside, rather than how you look on the outside. But by getting to know yourself better through the exercises in this book, maybe you've discovered that your current appearance doesn't match who you really are.

OUR EXPERIENCE OF IMAGE

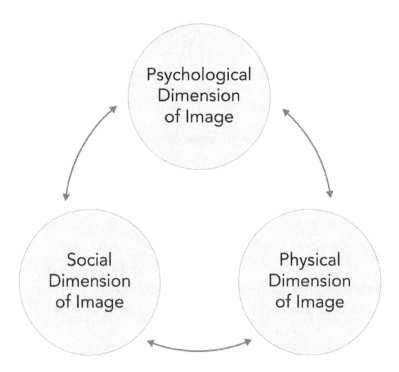

Think of three specific times when you went out in public over the past week. It might be to go to work, or to church, or to the grocery store. You might have been going to pick up your children from school or out to dinner with friends. Now assess your mindset in each of these instances. Did you have total confidence in your appearance? Did you leave your home knowing that you felt good on the inside and that feeling was reflected in your external appearance? If so, what was it about your appearance that you loved? What was it about your appearance that felt so congruent with how you were feeling on the inside? If not, what about your appearance felt wrong? What aspect of your true nature or your personality was missing?

The Association of Image Consultants International (AICI) lists three main areas of core competency for image consultants—the psychological aspects of image, the physical aspects of image, and the social aspects of image.

This diagram helps to show the relationships between our feelings and beliefs about our appearance (the psychological component) and our actual appearance (physical) and the feedback we receive regarding our appearance (the social aspect). The cycle goes in both directions, radiating out from our thoughts and feelings about ourselves. Our confidence influences not only how others see us, but also the actions we take that influence our physicality.

This cycle can represent an upward spiral where our healthy, self-affirming beliefs create helpful actions that result in a more vibrant physical appearance and thereby positive feedback from others. Positive feedback in the form of a compliment might then boost our confidence even further.

Where passion assassins are allowed to flourish, the opposite, downward spiral could also occur where negative beliefs create unhealthy decisions that affect our physical appearance and result in a negative vibe from others.

In the interest of embracing the upward spiral described above, let's examine our psyche for some image passion assassins.

Do any of the following thoughts have a trace of truth for you?

- I've styled my hair the same way for years. I'd like a change, but I don't know what to do with it.

- I think I'd look better with _____ (short hair, red hair, etc.), but my husband likes my hair _____ (long, blonde, etc.)
- I have the most boring wardrobe on the planet; it's full of frumpy, old wife/mother clothes.
- I have shirts (or shoes, or coats, or dresses) that are older than my teenage kids.
- I'd love to dress more fashionably, but I don't want to spend a fortune on clothes.
- I'd love to dress up more, but I never go anyplace where it would be appropriate.
- I'd love to dress more _____ (professionally, casually, fashionably, provocatively, etc.), but no one else dresses like that at my _____ (office, church, school, etc.).
- I'm so uncomfortable with my weight, but I've tried everything and can't take off the pounds.
- I know I would look and feel better if my level of fitness was better, but I just don't have the energy to work out like that.
- I look better with makeup, but I don't have time to spend on primping every day.
- I might look better with makeup, but I don't know how to put it on.
- I've been putting on the same makeup in the same shades for years.

With your Sexy Little Twist in full swing, you may decide that you are perfectly comfortable with your appearance, that how you currently look on the outside already speaks perfectly to who you are on the inside. Or you may decide that a makeover is in order.

If a makeover resonates with your heart, this chapter will help you get started, whether you're just wanting to make a few minor tweaks, or if you are going all-out and redoing everything, from your hairstyle to your wardrobe.

As with everything else in life, your appearance begins with your beliefs. When I began my journey to adding a little more ME back into my life, I realized that I had given up, in some ways, on my appearance. I had, in many ways, adopted OPEs for how I should look as a fortysomething wife and mother.

As I examined my excuses and my habits, I realized that some of these OPEs had become passion assassins for me, while other excuses and habits were sheer laziness on my part. As I got older, I told myself that no one was looking at me anyway, so why bother?

The truth that hit me as I went through my journey was that it wasn't at all about what others saw; it was about how I felt. *I* was looking—at myself in the mirror every day.

As I set about fulfilling my dreams of being a writer, coach, and retreat host, I needed photos for my website and business cards. A friend of mine, who is a professional photographer and also a very stylish woman, offered to take my photos and suggested I have my hair and makeup professionally done prior to the photo shoot.

Not at all sure that I would enjoy the experience, I cautiously agreed to the makeover. And all I can say is, "Wow!" If you haven't had a professional makeover before, do it now! The transformation that I saw in the mirror, and in the photos later, was nothing short of miraculous. And I wasn't the only one to notice. Everyone who saw those photos was astounded at how much better, younger, prettier, and more confident I looked.

After having that makeover done, I started to realize the nonsense I had been telling myself about my appearance. Things like, "I'm too old to wear the latest fashions" and "No one's looking anyway, so it doesn't matter how I dress."

Sure, I *looked* better when I had that makeover done, but the real eye-opener was how much better I *felt!* And that translated into a fresh outlook on my future—what I could still achieve, what I could still experience, and what I could still be. Discovering and eliminating a few of my appearance passion assassins opened my mind up to the possibility of discovering and eliminating other types of passion assassins.

So, before you skip this chapter with a casual, "Oh, I don't care about all of that external appearance stuff," do yourself a favor and at least consider the possibility that it might affect your mentality more than you realize. Take the time to explore the ideas presented here. If you still feel the same at the end of this chapter, then no harm done. But the mental and emotional boost you could end up experiencing as a result is well worth the time spent.

When I fully realized the connection between how I felt about my appearance and how I felt about achieving my dreams, I decided to learn as much as possible about enhancing my look. The best resource I have found thus far has been "The Makeover Guy," Christopher Hopkins. He has a helpful website (the makeoverguy.com) as well as a fabulous book, *Staging Your Comeback*, which is chockfull of information that every woman should know. Some of the highlights are included here. For more in-depth instructions, I highly recommend getting a copy of it.

As you go through this chapter, be mindful of any of the following passion assassins, which are likely beliefs you've picked up from other people, however well-meaning, throughout the course of your life:

- It's what's inside, not outside, that's important.
- Women should age gracefully.
- People should accept me for who I am, not how I look.
- Beauty is shallow.
- There are more important things in the world than how you look.
- Natural is better than "made-up."
- There are better uses for your money.
- Once you start, you have to maintain it.

And listen closely to your inner chatter for any of the following excuses:

- I'm just a stay-at-home mom.
- I'm a no-muss, no-fuss kind of gal.
- I don't have time.
- My husband doesn't like makeup.
- It's not a priority.
- No one dresses up in my town.
- I just want to be comfortable.
- I don't know how.
- It's too much work.
- I look better without all that makeup.

- No one sees me anyway.
- I can't afford to maintain it.
- I don't lift weights because I don't want to look muscular.
- I look better with more weight on as I age.
- I don't care what people think.
- That's just not me; I'm not one of those high-maintenance women.

"When how you appear reflects who you are, you are beautiful."
—Christopher Hopkins

Professional Opinions

In a book that encourages introspection and finding the answers within, I'm now going to recommend getting an outside opinion. There are a few areas of appearance where it helps to get the advice of a trained professional. This is due not only to their extensive training in the topic, but you may also find that your inner chatter has become so loud regarding your appearance that you have difficulty hearing your true self.

A color analysis can be done at numerous establishments, including salons, cosmetics shops, and cosmetics counters in department stores. Find out what colors make you appear more vibrant and healthy. Color analysis can help you select makeup, hair color, and clothing.

A good stylist can help you determine what hair styles look best with your face shape. They can also suggest styles that work well with your hair type and recommend products to make the most of it.

Instruction on how to properly apply makeup is available at many salons, cosmetics shops, and cosmetics counters at department stores as well. You are not alone if the idea of thousands of makeup options overwhelms you. A cosmetics professional can help you make the process as simple or as complex as you want it to be.

"You can be gorgeous at thirty, charming at forty,
and irresistible for the rest of your life."
—Coco Chanel

Your Personal Style

While an image consultant can help you determine your personal style, it's an area that you can absolutely figure out on your own if you choose. You can find many online resources for determining your style in the form of quizzes and questionnaires. I used the questionnaire in Christopher Hopkins' *Staging Your Comeback* book that I recommended previously. Knowing your personal style will help tremendously in finding hairstyles and clothing that work for you. It will also aid in making your clothing purchases more congruent so that when you bring a new piece home from a shopping trip, it will tend to work with other things already in your closet. Besides that, it's just fun!

Many of the personal style questionnaires I have found provide a handful of distinct image profiles. By answering questions about your preferences, you can zero in on your style and ultimately help you choose items that you'll feel and look great in. The questions usually center on the following areas:

- What are some words that describe your personality?
- Describe your dream or signature outfit.
- What would you wear to a cocktail party where you wanted to make a great impression?
- Describe your perfect hairstyle.
- What style of décor do you prefer for your living spaces?
- Describe a piece of jewelry that makes you look great.
- What celebrity do you admire for her sense of style?
- Describe the best compliment you could ever receive on your appearance.

Several of the questionnaires I have taken, including Hopkins', outlines six distinct image profiles—classic, casual or natural, romantic, dramatic, innovative or creative, and alluring. These profiles are not designed to box you in. You may find that, like me, your style spans two or more of these descriptions. Like everything else in this book, the questions are beneficial in helping you dig deep and find out what you really like and dislike. On that note, a word of advice about taking a personal style questionnaire—answer the questions according to what you *like* rather than how you are currently dressing. You might find that the current contents of your closet don't accurately represent who you really want to be.

> *"Being who you are is one thing, but letting others see who you are*
> *takes a little more thought. If you want to be appreciated for who*
> *you are, it helps to present those qualities in how you look."*
> **—Christopher Hopkins**

Your Body Type

Your next step in refreshing your image happens when you learn your body type and learn to clothe yourself in styles that not only fit your Personal Image Profile, but also create balance for you. Balance and symmetry are pleasing to the eye, so regardless of your shape or size, you can optimize your appearance with the proper application of cuts, colors, textures, and accents.

Determining your body type, horizontal and vertical, can truly simplify looking beautiful. Take the time to measure yourself if you haven't done this in a while . . . or, like me, ever.

Hopkins defines the four horizontal body types as: X (commonly known as the hourglass shape), A (triangle shape, with hips larger than bust and waist), Y (inverted triangle, with bust and back proportionally larger than waist and hips), and I (or rectangle—where waist, bust, and hips show little difference proportionally).

Here are instructions for determining your horizontal body type:

1. Measure around your bust at the nipples while wearing a regular bra (do not wear a padded or minimizer bra). My bust:_____.
2. Measure your waist. Circle your waist with a tape measure, pulling back and forth until it settles at the true waist, which is below the rib cage but above the navel. My waist:_____.

3. Measure your hips. Circle the tape measure around the fullest part of your hips as viewed from both the front and side. Usually this is around the fullest part of your butt at the hip bone. My hips:_____.

If your bust and hips measure approximately the same, and your waist is ten inches smaller (give or take an inch or two), you are an X. If your bust is smaller than your hips, you are an A. If your bust is larger than your hips, you are a Y. If your bust, waist and hips are similar in circumference, you are an I.

My horizontal body type is:_____.

While most women know their horizontal body type, the majority have never considered their vertical proportions. Are you long-legged and short-waisted? Do you have a long torso with shorter legs? There are lots of resources for determining your vertical body type, including Hopkins' easy-to-follow directions in his book, so I won't include them here.

But once you know these things, you can clothe your body to better enhance your look. You'll know what to avoid in wardrobe choices, such as long tunic styles if you have a long torso with shorter legs, and what to embrace, such as longer sweaters and tunic blouses if you have a shorter torso and longer legs.

> *"The most beautiful makeup of a woman is passion.*
> *But cosmetics are easier to buy."*
> **—Yves Saint-Laurent**

Self-Care

Another area where most women can easily add a Sexy Little Twist involves what are commonly thought of as personal indulgences—spa services such as manicures, pedicures, and facials, deep hair conditioning, teeth whitening, and the like. Are you paying attention to the appearance of your hands and feet? How about the health of your skin and hair? How about the brightness of your smile? Caring for yourself doesn't have to be expensive, as many things can be done at home, if you choose.

Try making it a priority to enhance the appearance of even one of these areas for a month and see how great you feel.

For your hands and feet, try purchasing a sixty-second sugar scrub and making it a habit to use it once a week. As soon as you've finished, spend a few minutes on your fingernails and toenails, whether you choose to trim and file and leave them natural or spend the extra time putting on some polish.

For your skin, get rid of products that aren't working for you or are outdated. Get into a daily routine of taking care of your skin, including staying hydrated and getting the right nutrients in your diet.

For your hair, try a weekly deep conditioner, even if it's one you concoct at home out of honey and olive oil. There are lots of recipes available on the Internet.

For your teeth, try one of the many over-the-counter options available now at your local market or drugstore. It's become far less expensive to keep your smile bright, and nothing says Sexy Little Twist better than a dazzling smile.

I would be remiss if I didn't mention fitness here. Making the most of our body type through clothing choices is one thing. Making the most of our body type through being in the best shape we can be is where the magic will really happen for you. If you know in your heart that the real you is two sizes smaller than where you are at the moment, then set that goal and start taking steps in that direction. Do what you need to do to become the best version of yourself. I cannot stress enough how profoundly it will impact all other areas of your life when you prove to yourself that you can achieve your ideal size.

A Vision of You

We created a vision for our health in Chapter 9, but I want to revisit that vision here in light of the concepts I've shared in this chapter. Take out your Sexy Little Twist journal. Spend a few minutes reviewing your vision for your health. Now set a timer for fifteen minutes and write an enhanced version of that vision, which includes how you're presenting yourself to the world. In your ideal vision of health and beauty:

- How much do you weigh and what size do you wear? How do your clothes feel on your body? Do you love getting dressed in the morning? Are you eating healthy foods and drinking plenty of water? Are you getting adequate exercise, both indoors and out? Are you flexible and energetic?

- What kinds of clothes are you wearing? What styles and colors of clothes are in your closet? Is your closet empty of old, outdated clothing? Is it full of new, fresh styles that just work on your body type? What fabrics are your clothes made from? Do they feel good to the touch? Do you regularly go through your clothes to get rid of things you're no longer wearing? Do you regularly replace your undergarments so that they're always in great shape?

- Do your hands and feet reflect the high level of self-love and self-respect that you feel? Are your nails trimmed and manicured? Are your feet soft and free of calluses?

- How about your skin? Is it soft and blemish free? Does it have a healthy glow to it from the adequate water you're drinking and the nutrients you're feeding your body? Do you have a regular routine for caring for your skin, including moisturizer and sun protection? Is it free of unsightly moles and skin tags?

- Is your hair healthy looking? Does your hairstyle really feel like YOU and make you feel good when you leave your house? Do you enjoy styling it in the morning? Are you in the habit of caring for your hair through weekly deep conditioning?

- How's your smile? Are your teeth as bright as they can be? Do you regularly whiten them? Do you get compliments on your smile?

- How about your makeup regimen? Are your cosmetics fresh and up-to-date? Do the colors you use look great on you? Does your foundation make you look more natural? Overall, does your makeup enhance your best features?

Once you've created this vision for your health and appearance, take the following steps:

- Review your entire vision on a regular basis—preferably daily, but weekly at a minimum.

- From your vision, select three top priorities for what you want to create in your life first and write an affirmation for each one. For example, if your top priority is to have a fabulous wardrobe, create an affirmation such as "My closet is full of clothes that I love and that look amazing on me."

- Repeat the affirmations on a regular basis, along with the affirmations you created in Chapter 12.

- Begin taking small steps, daily and weekly, that move you toward the reality of your affirmations. Using the example above, you might begin by getting rid of one piece of clothing each day, or even each week, that no longer speaks to the woman you've become.

Sexy Little Twists of Gorgeous

- Your life, with a Sexy Little Twist results in an outward appearance that reflects beautifully who you are on the inside.

- Looking good profoundly affects how you feel, which is key to achieving your dreams.

- The concept of physical appearance can be fraught with passion assassins and excuses.

- Getting clear on your image profile makes hair and clothing choices easier.

- Learn your body type in order to enhance your best features, save time and money, and always look your best.

- Appearance goals can be achieved in the same way as any other goal.

Girl Talk (or Journaling Exercises):

Spend a few moments contemplating your appearance—your wardrobe, hairstyle, hands, feet, skin, and smile. Think of one area where you've allowed passion assassins or excuses to keep you from appearing the way you'd like. Share your thoughts with the group.

Think of a time, preferably within the past few years, when you looked and felt great. What was it about your appearance that you loved and beautifully expressed who you are on the inside? Share your experience with the group, as well as one thing you could do to look and feel like that again.

Share with the group your results from the Image Profile Quiz you took in this chapter. What are the buzzwords you selected to help describe your style? Tell the group about an outfit you've worn in the past that was NOT your style. Describe an outfit that reflects your style beautifully, which you either own or would like to own.

Share with the group your three affirmations from the exercise above. Describe how you'll feel when these three goals are achieved. How will you present yourself in the world? How will it change how you feel on the inside?

Discuss how you will use the concepts in this chapter to elevate and improve your results and your life. Commit to repeating your appearance affirmations on a daily basis and being open to taking whatever actions you're inspired to take. Be prepared to discuss your experience at the next meeting.

Chapter 15

"Who Are You and What Have You Done with My Wife?"

"Have a great time, Mom. Just don't come back weird."
—**Katie Hulce** before her mom Sharon left for a transformational seminar

By this time in your life, you've established some long-term relationships, based on many years of experiences together. Your relationships with parents and siblings have likely fallen into a routine of interaction. You might be married, divorced, or married again. You may have children, young or grown, living at home or out on their own. You have friends, both lifelong and more recent. You have coworkers and fellow church and community members with whom you interact regularly. You probably have come to know your hair stylist and have even established acquaintance-level relationships with the staff at your local grocery store, dry cleaners, and auto service center.

In each of these relationships, your interaction, whether healthy, unhealthy, or neutral, likely follows a pattern.

When you begin to make changes to your beliefs, and, ultimately, your behavior, it may shake things up in your world for a time. Even making small changes forces us to step out of our comfort zone, at least until the new routine becomes a habit. Those changes may create inner turmoil for us, as well as turmoil in our environment, our "outer" world.

In this chapter, I want to discuss how to address the outer turmoil and drama that will undoubtedly occur when you begin to make changes. I want to give you some encouragement and some techniques to use to keep yourself motivated when you feel as if the people around you would rather you had stayed the same. And I want to share some techniques that will help not only maintain those relationships, but also bring them to a higher level than you previously experienced.

Some self-improvement gurus would have you discontinue, or limit, contact with friends or family members who seem to bring you down or discourage you from achieving your goals and dreams. While avoiding negative input is certainly an effective approach to remaking yourself, I'd like to challenge you to first look at these habitually negative interactions as opportunities.

A word about the extreme case—I am not advocating that you stay in an abusive relationship. If you are being abused, get out now! I would never suggest you continue to work on a relationship that puts you in danger. There are many organizations out there that are in place to help you out of this type of situation. Find one and use it!

Having said that, what I *am* suggesting is that the current status of your relationships is a direct result of your own thoughts, feelings, and actions in the past. Recognize that you are an equal contributor to the health, good or bad, of your existing relationships. It is quite possible, and indeed probable, that by changing yourself—your thoughts, feelings, and actions—you will dramatically change the nature of each of your relationships.

The following are some concepts that you'll want to consider as you're directing your Sexy Little Twist.

Your Outer World Reflects Your Inner World

"The world is a great mirror."
—Thomas Dreier

Your current relationships reflect the relationship you have had with yourself up until this point in your life. A simple example would be that someone with low self-respect might allow others to treat her disrespectfully. This could manifest in small ways, such as allowing your teenage children to watch television while you make six trips between the garage and kitchen, schlepping all the groceries in; or in large ways, such as accepting without protest a heavier share of the load at the office for less pay than your coworkers who contribute less.

If your inner dialogue has supported the idea that you aren't deserving of respect, then your relationships likely reflect that belief. As you change your inner world and your beliefs about yourself, your relationships will naturally change as a result. In the cases mentioned above, you might find yourself asking your teenagers to bring in the groceries and put them away while you get dinner started (which has the beautiful effect of raising your own self-respect while simultaneously raising theirs, even while they're grumbling about it). And you might find yourself presenting a valid proposal for a raise to your boss, which could possibly result in more income, but will definitely increase your self-respect and likely your boss's respect for you as well.

Realizing that your innermost thoughts, feelings, and beliefs actually create your reality is one of the most powerful lessons you can ever learn. It's a concept that seems scary at first. As in "Oh crap! You mean I actually created this mess?" But as you learn more, it dawns on you that this also means you can "uncreate" it, too. You can manifest a whole new experience that's decidedly unmessy!

To that end, I want to teach you the five most powerful words in personal growth and transformation. You ready for them? Here they are:

". . . because that's what I'm doing."

When you find yourself feeling frustrated, annoyed, hurt, angry, or any other negative emotion toward another person, as you think about what they do that frustrates, annoys, hurts, or angers you, finish the sentence in your head with ". . . because that's what I'm doing."

Ultimately, what we notice in others' behavior reflects how we're feeling about ourselves. Have you ever noticed that you were annoyed at someone for some small offense, like cutting you off in traffic, and then realized that you had recently done the same thing to someone else, however inadvertently?

I noticed early in adulthood that I was most impatient with people who exhibited behaviors that I myself was struggling to overcome. For example, it used to drive me crazy, and sometimes still does, when I see someone who allows other people to take advantage of them and avoids standing up for themselves. I realized that it annoyed me so badly to see other people do this because I had the same bad habit. Now, when I find myself getting annoyed because someone is allowing another person to take advantage of them, I can state it in my head as, "I'm really annoyed at so-and-so for letting so-and-so take advantage of her, because that's what I'm doing." And I can stop and consider:

- How and where am I allowing someone to take advantage of me?
- Where in my life do I need to do a better job of standing up for myself?

So you see, when we experience negative emotions about someone else's behavior, we can count on it that who we're really frustrated, annoyed, or disappointed in is ourselves.

Now you might be saying, "But what if they really are being an asshole?" The truth? If you've dealt with your own inner conflict about the behavior, you'll still notice that someone is being an asshole; it just won't have the power to upset, frustrate, annoy, anger, or disappoint you. You'll recognize the behavior for what it truly is—their issue. And it'll roll right off of you like a forgotten cup of coffee off the roof of your car, only without the mess.

Try this exercise now for practice. Take out your Sexy Little Twist journal and spend a few minutes writing your thoughts on the following:

1. _____ (person's name) really _____ (frustrates, annoys, disappoints, angers, etc.) me when he/she _____

_____.

2. When he/she does this, I feel _____ (disrespected, unappreciated, taken advantage of, unimportant, used, etc.).

3. This really_____ (frustrates, annoys, disappoints, angers, etc.) me because that's what I do when I _____

_____.

4. Three actions that I can take to avoid this in the future are:
   a. _____.
   b. _____.
   c. _____.

For example:

1. My boss really angers me when she gives me work to do at the last minute and expects me to work over my weekend to get it done in time. She knew about the project days ago and should've given me more notice. She does this all the time!
2. When she does this, I feel disrespected and unappreciated.
3. This really angers me because that's what I do when I accept the project without telling her how I really feel. I'm disrespecting myself, and I'm not showing the proper appreciation for my own time.
4. Three actions I can take to avoid this in the future are:
   a. I'll schedule an appointment with my boss as soon as possible and explain, calmly and respectfully, how I feel about repeatedly having to work on my weekends to complete last-minute requests.
   b. I'll request that she show me more respect and appreciation by allowing me adequate time to get projects finished during the work week.
   c. If, after this meeting, she continues to drop projects on me at the last minute, then I will consider the merits of just saying "no", or I

will continue to complete her requests until I find another position elsewhere.

You can use this simple exercise to work through just about any negative situation that you're experiencing. If you'd like to get more in depth, check out Byron Katie's book *The Work*. Katie teaches people to explore and examine their innermost thoughts and feelings in great detail, to look at them as dispassionately as you would a rock. This ultimately results in the greatest inner peace you could ever experience.

Give It Time

Appreciate that your relationship patterns weren't established overnight; neither should you anticipate them being corrected overnight. Understand that some things can take time. If you have been in an adversarial relationship with a coworker or one of your children or step-children, and you begin to change how you interact with them based on a sincere desire to improve communication, then recognize that there may be some lingering distrust on their part. If you stay the course, they will eventually come to accept and trust the new you. Just smile and think to yourself, "They'll be along shortly." As you learn to accept where you are in your own life journey, you'll develop a respect for the fact that others are where they are on their journey as well.

Take the First Step

Even if "he started it," realize that you may have to be the one to take that first conciliatory step toward the other person. He or she may or may not be in the same place you are in terms of wanting or being willing to make changes. If the relationship is important enough to you that you're still hanging in there, then maybe it's important enough that you can let go of needing to be right about who caused the rift or tension in the first place.

This issue is mostly about being vulnerable. In a relationship that has become mostly negative, we are on guard. We don't put our true feelings out there for fear of them being stomped on—again. In reality, this never works. By doing this, we hide our true nature for fear that we'll be rejected. Refer back to Chapter 12 where we affirmed that "we would rather be loathed for who we really are than loved for who we are not."

Acknowledge that you are the only one you can change. Period. End of story. There is nothing you can do to *make* the other person even *want* to change, let alone actually make them change. Having said that, as you focus on becoming a more peaceful, happy, purposeful, and passionate person, others will definitely notice. And in the case of the relationships worth saving, they'll follow your lead.

Feedback in Relationships

Jack Canfield shares a simple, but powerful technique in his book *The Success Principles*. This technique can be used in any relationship that you would like to improve—marital, professional, parental, friendship, etc. You simply ask the other person a series of questions, actively listen to their responses, and take small steps to implement their suggestions. If you'll make it a weekly habit, then your relationship can't help but improve. The questions are as follows:

1. On a scale of 1 to 10, how would you rate our relationship over the past week?
2. Whatever the response, ask, "Why so high?" This puts momentary focus on what's going well in the relationship, which encourages a discussion of actions you'll want to continue to take. For example, if they rate the relationship a 2, you would ask, "Why so high? Why is it not a 1?" Then listen to the answers and make a commitment to yourself to keep up those behaviors.
3. After discussing a few positive elements of your relationship, you then ask, "What would it take to make it a 3?" Jack asks, "What would it take to make it a 10?", but I'd suggest baby steps if it's less than a 6 or 7. Once you get a 7 or 8 response to this question, you can start asking what it would take to get to 10. If it's at a 2 and you ask what it would take to make it a 10, then you may get a rather discouraging earful of suggestions. Asking what it would take to improve incrementally will provide you with a small suggestion or two that you could incorporate into your routine more easily. Commit to working on something and

then *follow through*. And I can't stress enough the importance of the follow-through. Failure to take action here will result in a loss of trust and could make things worse than if you had never asked. Following through on even a small suggestion will increase trust (improving your own self-trust, as well as increasing the other person's trust in you). This is certainly a step in the right direction for a faltering relationship.

And that's it. Ask the three questions, listen to the answers with a genuine desire to fix things, and take small steps toward a better relationship.

A word of caution—at the start of this process, avoid asking for an equal commitment. Simply ask the questions, make the commitment, and do not expect anything in return. If your relationship has been negative for some time, your efforts likely will be met with resistance, and even suspicion, from the other party ("Oh, she's just manipulating me to try to get me to_____"). Keep at it for several weeks, always following through on what you've committed to. Patience and perseverance are keys to changing the course of a faltering relationship. They'll come around, or they won't. What they think, feel, or do isn't your concern or your responsibility.

And I mean that last bit—even if it's your spouse, you are not responsible for how they feel. This is a tough one for many women to grasp, but it's true. Just as your feelings are your responsibility, so are everyone else's feelings their own responsibility.

A New Way of Interacting

All of this could ultimately result in a new pattern of interaction in your relationships. As you become more comfortable with who you are, you tend to allow other people to be who they are as well. That's not to say that you'll always agree with the actions and behaviors of others, but it won't tend to frustrate, annoy, or anger you as much as it used to. Things will tend to roll off of you without any adverse effects. You won't give a strong, negative meaning to the things that happen around you, comments that people make, or things that people do. You'll come to understand that these things are not so much about you, but about the people who say and do them. Even in the case where a person makes a derogatory statement toward you, you'll know that this is really about them, not you.

This tracks with the concept that the world reflects back how we see ourselves. A simple demonstration is to think of how you would feel if someone walked up to you and said, "I don't like your purple hair," when your hair is clearly brown. Would you feel insulted? No, you'd probably just think they were crazy, or maybe color blind, and not give it another thought.

But if that same person walked up to you and said, "I don't like your selfishness," then how would you feel? The way you answer this question is very telling. If you chose to feel insulted, then you'd want to examine your deepest beliefs about yourself, because somewhere in your mind and heart is the fear that they're right. If someone calls you selfish, and you know in your heart that you are not, then that insult would bounce off of you as easily as a comment about your purple hair when you know your hair is brown.

Another example of this is when someone honks their horn or makes a rude finger gesture at you while you're stuck in traffic. Does their behavior say more about you or about them? Of course, it says more about them. Have you ever been on the other side of this exchange where you're the one making the rude gesture? What was your state of mind at the time? Were you running late? Frustrated? Ticked off about something that happened that morning at home? Do you have incontrovertible evidence that the other driver was an inconsiderate lunatic, or is it possible that they were distracted or running late or even just got some horrific news that caused them to be less than attentive to their surroundings? It may be a twinge painful to think about it this way, but if you'll allow it, you'll learn something about yourself in the process.

Growing Through Overcoming Adversity

By this time in your life, you likely have already recognized the truth in this, but it's worth stating. We grow by overcoming adversity. It's true in terms of our own personal growth, and it's true in terms of our relationships.

A friendship that has lasted through rough times is far more solid and stable and, frankly, more beautiful than a friendship based on shared good times alone. Keep this in mind as you experience challenges in your relationships. While you're on your path to making changes in your life, there's really good stuff waiting on the other side of that adversity. Don't give up too easily.

A Word about "Toxic" People

There are lots of terms for it out there—toxic people, emotional vampires, and such. These terms refer to people who always seem to drain your energy and steal your positive emotions. If you're familiar with the *Harry Potter* series, think of a *dementor*—in their presence, all your joy and happiness just gets sucked right out of you.

While I'm not sure I buy into the idea that a person can be toxic (I tend to think everyone just has their own unexamined, unresolved crap), I do believe that some relationships may have to be left behind, sometimes temporarily, sometimes permanently, in order for you to become your best version of YOU and fulfill your life purpose.

Like an alcoholic fresh out of rehab, you might need to step away from unhealthy, negative influences while you're still wobbling on these Sexy new legs of yours.

For me, however, this is a last resort after applying the methods above. You'll grow in self-respect and self-trust through examining and transforming your own thoughts and behavior first. When you're self-assured, confident, and have a fantastic relationship with yourself, you'll naturally know what you need to do when it comes to your relationships with others.

The Importance of Uplifting Friendships

In your quest to make changes in your life, it's best to have some company. This does not include those relationships that we discussed above—the ones you're trying to salvage, with people who aren't quite supportive or convinced just yet of your commitment to change. Nope. I'm talking about people in any one (or more) of the following categories:

- Those who have always been completely supportive of you and your efforts.

- Those people you know (or know of) who are just generally positive, uplifting types.
- People who are in the same situation and at the same stage as you, making a fresh commitment to change their lives.
- People who already have accomplished what you want to accomplish.

A critical component of living your life with a Sexy Little Twist is surrounding yourself with positive, uplifting, supportive people, who will help you stay inspired and motivated on your journey. These are the people you'll go to when you're in need of a pep talk, and who you'll give a pep talk to when they need it.

The first step is to establish who's already in your corner by making a list of everyone that you hang around with. This includes the friend you chat with on the phone, who you follow on social media, who you work with, go to church with, have occasional drinks or coffee with, your family, your friends, and everyone you regularly come into contact with. So pull out your Sexy Little Twist journal and make that list. Go ahead, I'll wait . . . Finished? Great!

Now place a "+" or a "-" next to each person's name, indicating whether they are a positive force in your life or a negative one. Ask yourself if, after a visit or chat with them, you feel lifted or drained. Don't overthink it; just go with your gut on each one. If you tend to feel down or depressed when you're around them, then write a "-" next to their name. If you tend to feel uplifted and energetic in their company and after you leave them, then write a "+" next to their name.

The ones you've placed a "+" next to are the people you want to put yourself in the presence of, as much as possible, as you're giving your life a Sexy Little Twist. These are the people who bring out the best in you, the ones who remind you of who you want to be, who you are on the inside.

I realize that some of your close relationships—perhaps a spouse, parent, child, sibling, or close friend—may be on the "-" list. That's okay. If it's a relationship worth saving, the efforts you deploy from the above list will take care of things. As you uncover and reveal your true, authentic self, while allowing others to be who they are, the relationships with a foundation of mutual respect and love will strengthen. The ones that are not will fade into the background. You won't need to focus on eliminating negative relationships. In fact, focusing on them will only make them more prominent in your life. By focusing on bringing back your best self, you will bring the best relationships to the forefront of your life.

So regarding the positive relationships, the ones you put a "+" next to, make a commitment right now to spend more time with these people! Here are a few suggestions for making that happen.

- Establish a regular lunch or phone call with a person who is always supportive of you. I've made it a habit to call my dad every Monday morning. I respect and admire the way he always has and continues to live his life. He's always in my corner, and he has a wicked funny sense of humor that never fails to put me in a good mood. (I like to think our conversations brighten his day as well.) No worries if your parent isn't that person for you; whoever your parents are (or were), they're doing (or did) the best they can with what they know. Just realize who supports you and make an effort to be around them—a lot.

- Make an effort to get to know the people on your list whom you don't see frequently. Maybe it's someone from your work or church whose attitude you admire or someone you've clicked with in the past. Invite them to lunch or ask them over for dinner. Is it possible that it will be awkward at first? Yep. Do it anyway. Remember that you're a fascinating person, too, with a lot to offer a friend.

- If it's a person who has already achieved something that you want to achieve, ask them to consider mentoring you for a short time. Or offer to buy them lunch or a drink. Or offer to give them a ride to the airport the next time they travel in exchange for picking their brain en route. Don't be shy; most people are happy to share what they know.

- Start a Sexy Little Twist Book Club or Mastermind group. Okay, there's my plug for my own book, but the point is still a good one. Gather some people who have the same goal that you do—dusting off that vibrant, amazing person you've been hiding—and meet weekly or monthly to help each other through the process and celebrate your successes together. Mastermind groups are a great way for like-minded people to support each other in achieving their dreams.

• Assess your social media followings. Start following people and pages that give you an emotional boost each day and get rid of those that bring you down. There's no room in your camp and no time in your day for people who use social media to spew endless bitter complaints about their humdrum lives on anyone who will listen.

• Read uplifting books, blogs, magazines, etc. Get regular positive ideas flowing through your mind. Listen to audios in your car and make it a habit to read something positive at least fifteen minutes every day. This lifts your spirits in the moment and has the added benefit of increasing your knowledge over the long haul.

The bottom line? Keep your focus on your own improvement opportunities and watch your existing relationships improve little by little as you better your relationship with yourself. And give yourself a boost toward success by surrounding yourself with uplifting, positive people who inspire and encourage you to keep moving toward your dreams.

Sexy Little Twists of Relating

• Temporary turmoil is common and expected in your relationships when you set about making changes to your beliefs and actions.

• The current status of your relationships is a direct result of your own thoughts, feelings, and actions in the past.

• Your current relationships reflect the relationship you've had with yourself in the past.

• The five most powerful words in personal transformation are ". . . because that's what I'm doing."

• A key to living your life with a Sexy Little Twist is surrounding yourself with positive, uplifting, supportive people who help you stay motivated and inspired.

Girl Talk (or Journaling Exercises):

Think of a time when you were annoyed or frustrated with someone and then realized that you were really annoyed or frustrated with yourself. Share your experience with the group, as well as how you took, or will take, steps to avoid the frustration in the future.

Think of a relationship in your life that could use improvement. Discuss with the group ways, however small, that you have contributed to the poor state of your interactions, or lack thereof. Share one action that you could take to move the relationship in the right direction.

Name one person in your life who supports and lifts you. Discuss ways you might let them know your appreciation and ways you might go about increasing the time you spend with them.

Name one person you admire for their positive enthusiasm and/or achievements in life. Discuss ways you might go about spending more time with them.

Discuss how you will use the concepts in this chapter to elevate and improve your results and your life. Commit to one small change that you will make in your daily or weekly habits and be prepared to discuss your experience at the next meeting.

Chapter 16

Fill One Champagne Glass Every Day

"We are what we repeatedly do. Excellence, then, is not an act but a habit."
—Aristotle

A t this time, you may be plagued by concerns about slipping backward and losing all of the progress you've made as you've worked through the exercises in this book. Let me reassure you that if you've diligently completed the exercises outlined here, you have *become* different than you were before; you have become more YOU. And therefore, it isn't possible for you to go back to being the woman you were before, because you *know* things now that you didn't know then. You are wiser, and you are more in touch with your true self. Not because of what I've shared with you, but because of the introspection you've done and the discoveries you've made about yourself since picking up this book.

Having said that, I do want to leave you with some parting words about how to maintain your newfound lease on life more easily.

Making real, lasting changes to your life becomes SO much easier through the power of rituals and habits. By developing rituals and habits, we effectively manage our precious energy and translate our purpose, vision, and priorities into action. Through habits based on our purpose and vision, we overcome the limitations of our willpower and self-discipline.

With that in mind, I want to share my own personal method for sustaining progress and continued growth. This little poem and acronym represent my daily rituals that keep me moving toward my dreams. You ready for it? It's a little thing I like to call:

MAGAVER5

It's based on the little things I do daily that keep me moving confidently and determinedly in the direction of my dreams. It started as a way to remember all of the things I wanted to do each day in my quest to transform my life. Knowing that my mind retains things better if they rhyme, I wrote an embarrassingly silly poem so that I'd remember them all. At the risk of revealing my inner dork, here is the original poem that MAGAVER5 is based upon:

"Meditate, Affirmate,
Gratitude, Appreciate,
Value Add, Exercise,
Read and 5, Dreams Realize!"

These are the eight things I do daily to keep myself moving forward, to keep myself on track for achieving what I want, to live my life with a Sexy Little Twist of ME. Wanting to simplify things even further, I created the acronym MAGAVER5 from the poem. Each letter and number represents one of my daily habits. Let me break it down for you.

Meditate

As I've said before, I know of no better way to stay in touch with myself, with my true heart's desires, than to meditate regularly. It doesn't even matter if you're terrible at it. I certainly don't claim to be an expert, but I can't tell you how much benefit I get out of this practice. Even on the days when my mind keeps jumping to all the things I need to get done, I end my meditation with a much calmer, peaceful, more organized mindset than when I started. I never realized how shallow my breathing was until I started meditating. Try relaxing sometime while you're breathing short, shallow breaths. It's not easy.

Meditation gives us a quiet break from our often chaotic lives; it reduces stress, helps clarify decisions, and more. It's a gift we can give ourselves each day that reinforces the importance of self-care.

It's also a great source of inspiration. Do you ever get great ideas in the shower? Well, meditation is like that, only without having to shave your legs at the same time. You can get all sorts of creative ideas and intuitions while you sit quietly and just "be."

Affirmate

Okay, so I took a little creative license and made up a word. By "affirmate," I mean that each day I review my goal affirmations or Double Secret Agents (DSAs), which I've turned into a four-minute photo collage set to music. I watch and listen to my affirmation movie, visualizing all the amazing things I want to create in my life. Along with visualizing, I *feel* the feelings of having achieved all of my goals—the joy, the peace, the fun, and the love of experiencing all of my dreams.

In addition to simply feeling great, doing this sets my mind to work on figuring out how to make things happen. Throughout the day, and through my meditation, I get lots of little inspired ideas for actions I can take to move toward what I've affirmed.

Gratitude

Each day, I encourage myself to live in a state of gratitude by writing five things in my Gratitude Journal. It takes just a few minutes of my time, but does wonders for my attitude, my outlook, and my productivity.

Sometimes I write small things for which I'm grateful, like my iPhone, which helps me stay organized (mostly). Sometimes I write big things, like the good health of my kids. Regardless, big or small, trifling or significant, the feeling and the result is the same. Though I only write five, my eyes open up to many, many more things for which to be grateful. And here's a tip that I didn't discover until well into my Sexy Little Twist journey—for HUGE benefits from a Gratitude Journal, remember to include the challenges and opportunities! Write in your journal how grateful you are that your husband forgot your birthday, because it gave you the opportunity to realize how much you've grown in self-love and self-confidence, and the opportunity to grow even more. Be grateful for that flat tire because it gave you the opportunity to practice patience and inner calm.

And be grateful for the small things. If you've seen the film *The Secret*, then you may recall Joe Vitale, who was once homeless, describing how he became grateful for a #2 pencil. He didn't have much, so he began by being grateful for what little he did have access to. With a pencil, he realized he could fill out a job application, write a love letter, or begin writing a book. He was surprised, when he really thought about it, just how amazingly helpful a pencil could be.

You have access to countless things in your life, which may be going unnoticed. However you choose to cultivate gratitude in your life, whether through a journal, a visual cue such as a sticky note on your dashboard, or a piece of jewelry you wear often, make it a daily practice and watch the amazing results.

Appreciate

It's one thing to be grateful for someone or something, but it's quite another to express it out loud. I've made it a habit to acknowledge and appreciate at least one person each day for something they've done for me or for others. This can take the form of a verbal thank you (in person or over the phone), an email, a Facebook message, or a card.

When you implement this practice into your life, you'll see how powerful this small step is in making someone's day. So many people spend much of their life feeling unappreciated. Help tip the scales on that by telling someone every day how much you appreciate them.

The best acknowledgements are specific—

- To a friend: "I really appreciate how you always make me laugh when I'm feeling frustrated."
- To a child: "I noticed you took out the garbage without being asked. I really appreciate the self-discipline you're developing."
- To the cashier at the grocery store: "Thanks so much for the great service. With this many items, I was expecting it to take a lot longer than it did."

If you're not accustomed to doing this on a regular basis, it may feel awkward in the beginning. It may feel wooden at first, like you're simply trying to check something off your list. No worries! Keep at it, and very quickly it will begin to feel completely natural. You'll soon be acknowledging and appreciating people without even realizing you're doing it.

Value Add

Right after I write down the five things I'm grateful for each day, I then write three things that I did the previous day to *add value*. As you know from Chapter 8 where you discovered your life purpose, real fulfillment in life comes when we put our talents to use in serving others. The simple act of recognizing and recording how you contributed to the betterment of others keeps you in touch with this essential part of your nature.

Your list of "Value Adds" might include:

- Cooking dinner for your family
- Visiting a relative in a nursing home
- Finishing a project at work
- Posting some helpful content on social media
- Doing some volunteer work
- Encouraging a friend
- Developing a new product or service
- Sharing a fresh idea in a meeting

It doesn't matter if the actions are small or large, only that it was in some way helpful to others. This activity is a self-confidence booster, as it encourages us to realize on a daily basis that our actions matter to others as well as ourselves. It can also help us to recognize our contribution from a financial perspective, reminding us of our value to employers or clients—a tremendous asset when it's time to set pricing for our services or ask for a raise from our boss.

Exercise

Nothing earth-shattering here, but simply a commitment to getting my body moving each and every day, to stay as fit as possible. Living my life with a Sexy Little Twist means, among other things:

- Having the energy to get out of bed with enthusiasm and maintain that excitement throughout the day.
- Staying healthy and avoiding illnesses, minor or major, so that when I take a day off to relax and rejuvenate, it's because I want to, not because I have to.
- Feeling and looking good in clothes that I love.
- Reminding myself on a daily basis the importance of taking care of myself and spending a little time out in the fresh air.
- Having time to myself each day, so that I can hear myself think and allow my creativity free rein.
- Feeling a sense of accomplishment each night when I go to bed, as if I've moved a little closer to my dreams and goals.
- Maintaining an optimistic outlook on my life, my future, my ability to fulfill my purpose, and the inevitability of living my life vision.

Daily exercise helps me to achieve all of this and more. I've also found that *not* exercising has a reverse effect, causing a backward slide in many of these areas. When I neglect my physical health for any period of time, my mental and emotional health also suffers.

So why let that happen, when it's so easy to turn it around? It's not even about working out for an hour a day; you can gain all of these benefits in fifteen minutes, or even less, of physical activity. Get down on the floor and do some ab crunches and push-ups. Ride that dusty stationary bike while you're watching

TV or reading. Go for a quick walk before or after dinner. Incorporate exercise into other activities you're doing anyway, like housework or driving. A study showed that hotel housekeeping staff lost weight and achieved other health-related benefits simply by learning to think of their daily activities as exercise. No change in activity was even necessary, only how they *thought* about it!

If you're active already, fabulous! Keep up the great work! If you realize that your health, mental and physical, could benefit from a little more movement on your part, put this book down right now and give me twenty! Seriously, put the book down and do twenty ab crunches right now. Then, do them again tomorrow. And the next day. And the next. You'll be living your life with a Sexy Little Twist in no time!

Read

Each day, I make it a habit to read something positive, uplifting, educational, and/or inspirational for a minimum of fifteen minutes. This is a daily habit that, rather than struggling to squeeze it in, I usually have to force myself to stop and get something else done. I absolutely love to read and could (and sometimes do) spend hours upon hours engulfed in a well-written book, learning something new or learning to look at something I already knew in a whole new way.

When I set out to learn what was possible through personal transformation, I read book after book on the topic and have presented only some of the highlights here in this book you're holding. There is a world of knowledge out there, on every topic you can think of, and it's all readily available to you through books and blogs and magazines.

I've always been fascinated with the self-taught, self-made person. I love the idea of setting out to become an expert on something and doing just that through a self-directed educational pursuit. In what area would you like to become an expert? Archeology? Salsa dancing? Geology? Classic literature? Wine . . . or vodka? Quilting? Finance? Leadership? Asian culture? French cuisine? The architecture of Florence, Italy? I read a book recently that's a byproduct of a woman taking it upon herself to read more than forty books on organizing and cleaning her house. She became an expert in the process and now has a wildly successful book of her own. Whatever it is for you—whatever stirs your passion, or even a mild curiosity—it's all right there at your fingertips, ready for you to devour! How exciting!

Aside from the benefits of pursuing a passion and becoming an expert at something you love, reading educational and inspirational material helps to:

- Keep you in an open frame of mind so that you can see the myriad of possibilities around you.
- Lift your mood.
- Keep your brain healthy and ward off age-related deterioration.
- Put you in the perfect state of mind for experiencing restful, restorative, and productive sleep.

In addition, reading positive, uplifting material helps to augment your new goal of surrounding yourself with positive, uplifting people. When you begin your adventure of showing up Fashionably Late to your life, you may feel that you're struggling to remain in a positive, confident, and optimistic state of mind. You may feel as if you're surrounded by remnants of your less-than-sexy past behavior. When your environment and your relationships have not yet caught up with your new Sexy Little Twist on life, the encouraging and inspiring words of others on the page can be the little boost you need to keep going in the right direction. As with other daily rituals, even fifteen minutes is enough to get all the benefits.

5–The Rule of 5

And this, my friends, is where the rubber meets the road in your Sexy Little Twist of Fate. This is where your dreams are translated into your reality. Don't go to bed without having taken five actions, however small or large, toward your dreams. The most impactful way to use this is for all five actions to be targeted specifically toward your Twist of Fate goal.

This book you have in your hands is the direct result of the successful use of the Rule of 5. I made the decision that I wouldn't stop until I realized my dream of publishing a book, and then, with a few exceptions, I took five actions every day toward that dream. What amazing creation is inside of you, waiting to be brought forth and shared with the world? Apply the Rule of 5 to your dreams and find out! I can't wait to see what it is!

So those are my daily rituals. Each one has its own impact on my ability—physical, mental, emotional, and spiritual—to live my life with a Sexy Little Twist, to show up Fashionably Late to my own life. Aside from the Rule of 5, I can get all of these habits accomplished in just a little over one hour. Completing my Rule of 5 takes a little longer, depending on what I have on my list for that day.

You may be thinking "Where the hell am I going to find an hour in my day?" I want you to go back to your Sexy Little Twist journal and read your vision again. Then ask yourself, "Would I give up one hour of my day in order to live that life?" If the answer is "No," then revise your vision—it's not sexy enough yet. If the answer is "Yes," you'll find a way.

Try MAGAVER5 for thirty days. Keep track of your progress in your Sexy Little Twist journal. At the end of thirty days, make adjustments to it as you see fit, but make sure that your mind, body, and spirit all are being nurtured every day.

So, one final question for you as you close this book and get busy making your dreams come true—Who's Sexy Now?

That's right, girlfriend, YOU are!

Sexy Little Twists of Habit

- Using acronyms is helpful in remembering your daily success habits.
- Making lasting, impactful changes is easier through the power of habit and ritual.
- Acknowledging and appreciating others is a great way to give their day a boost, as well as your own.
- Becoming an expert on anything through self-directed study is Very Sexy!

Girl Talk (or Journaling Exercises):

Share with the group a daily habit or ritual that you had prior to reading this book. In what ways does it help you maintain and/or improve your physical, mental, emotional, and/or spiritual energy?

Think of a time in the past week when you acknowledged and appreciated someone. Describe the interaction to the group. How did the recipient of your praise react? How did you feel afterward? Discuss with the group other opportunities (whom and how) for you to acknowledge others in the upcoming weeks.

Think of an area or topic in which you would LOVE to become an expert. Share the topic with the group and spend some time brainstorming on various actions you might take in order to become an expert on it.

Discuss how you will use the concepts in this chapter to elevate and improve your results and your life. Commit to continuing the daily practice of MAGAVER5 for the full thirty-day period. Commit to the other members of the group to support each other in your continued Sexy Little Twist efforts, whether through ongoing meetings, group or individual conference calls, a Facebook group, or any other method you devise.

About the Author

Danne Reed is out to change the world, one late bloomer at a time. She inspires women to discover their gifts, celebrate who they are, and finally show up in the world as the amazing, passionate, confident person they always knew they could be. Her own journey took her from pouting over missing the party of life to dusting herself off and showing up fashionably late for it. She now teaches others—through her writing, speaking, coaching, retreats, and online programs—how to do the same.

CPSIA information can be obtained at www.ICGtesting.com
Printed in the USA
BVOW08s1423171115

427445BV00011B/336/P